Praise for *Leadership by Choice*

"Successful people never stop working to grow their influence as an effective, productive, and trustworthy leader. This book lays the groundwork to position you along the pathway that so many great leaders have traveled before you. Apply these proven strategies to your professional life and watch your career flourish."

—Dr. Nido Qubein
President, High Point University;
Chairman, Great Harvest Bread Co.

"If your aim as a leader is to be more effective, influence and persuade others, and get better results in your position, this book will show you the way."

—Brian Tracy
Author of *How the Best Leaders Lead*

"Leadership is not just about what you do but what you can inspire, encourage, and empower others to do. This is why I encourage you to read Eric's book. It's a road map for making the right choices to lead more powerfully and effectively!"

—Jon Gordon
Best-selling author of *The Energy Bus* and *Soup*

"If you have ever thought about leadership or consider yourself a leader, *Leadership by Choice* is a must read. Eric does a great job at combining entertaining stories with practical application you can use professionally and personally."

—Jack Canfield
Coauthor of the *Chicken Soup for the Soul* series
and *The Success Principles*

"*Leadership by Choice* offers practical application on how leaders can be more productive. Eric teaches leaders to align their strategic objectives with their day-to-day priorities."

—Laura Stack
President of the National Speakers Association,
America's premier expert in productivity;
Author of *What to Do When There's Too Much to Do*

"Leadership, as Eric Papp points out, is always a choice. And that choice begins within, getting in touch with who you are, what you care about, and what you are willing to do. Make that choice to lead—*and* read this book because it is full of wisdom (which is practical advice based on experience!). No matter where you are in your leadership journey, you'll find some good ideas in this book that can make you an even better leader."

—Barry Z. Posner, PhD,
Accolti Professor of Leadership,
Santa Clara University;
Coauthor of *The Leadership Challenge,*
Credibility, and *The Truth about Leadership*

"Whether leading at work, selling, or parenting, this book is golden, with a plethora of practical insights and how to's. Well done. Everyone in our company will benefit from reading this book."

—Cary Mullen
CEO VivoResorts.com, Oceanfront Properties

"Business is about people—always has been and always will be. *Leadership by Choice* provides page after page of practical insight about how to lead people to become the best version of themselves.

Unless you can do that your organization will never become the best version of itself."

—Matthew Kelly
New York Times bestselling author
of *The Dream Manager* and *Off Balance*

"If you can only buy one leadership book that will make a difference in your life—this is the one."

—Rocky Bleier
Vietnam Veteran;
4-time Superbowl Champion
with the Pittsburgh Steelers

LEADERSHIP

BY

CHOICE

Increasing Influence
and Effectiveness
through Self-Management

ERIC PAPP

WILEY

John Wiley & Sons, Inc.

Published by John Wiley & Sons, Inc., Hoboken, New Jersey.
Published simultaneously in Canada.

For general information on our other products and services or for technical support, please contact our Customer Care Department within the United States at (800) 762-2974, outside the United States at (317) 572-3993 or fax (317) 572-4002.

Wiley publishes in a variety of print and electronic formats and by print-on-demand. Some material included with standard print versions of this book may not be included in e-books or in print-on-demand. If this book refers to media such as a CD or DVD that is not included in the version you purchased, you may download this material at http://booksupport.wiley.com. For more information about Wiley products, visit www.wiley.com.

Library of Congress Cataloging-in-Publication Data:
Papp, Eric, 1983–
  Leadership by Choice: Increasing Influence and Effectiveness
through Self-Management / Eric Papp.
  1 online resource.
  ISBN: 978-1-118-29319-5 (cloth)
  ISBN: 978-1-118-33182-8 (ebk)
  ISBN: 978-1-118-33400-3 (ebk)
  ISBN: 978-1-118-33514-7 (ebk)
  1. Leadership. 2. Organizational effectiveness. 3. Communication in management.
4. Decision making. I. Title.
  HD57.7
  658.4'012–dc23

                                                            2012006629

Printed in the United States of America
10 9 8 7 6 5 4 3 2 1

To my father and mother,
Alex and Cindy Papp.
Thank you for your unconditional love,
support, and belief in me.

Contents

Acknowledgments

No man is an island, entire of itself; every man is a piece of the continent, a part of the main.

—John Donne

Many folks have been instrumental in my life and played a role in the completion of this book.

I want to first thank God. My motto has always been AMDG, which stands for "To the greater glory of God."

To my parents, Alex and Cindy, for believing in me, showing me the right path in life, and giving the two greatest gifts a parent can give: unconditional love and a strong work ethic.

To my brothers, Christopher and Jonathan, for their continued support and camaraderie.

To all of my audience members and clients, your outcomes, success, and feedback are why I do what I do. Thank you for putting your trust in me and being a partner in business.

To my friends in the National Speakers Association who have been instrumental in helping me over the years. Speaking can be a lonely business, and you make it enjoyable.

To the men and women in the military who allow us to enjoy a life of freedom.

To my editors, Cynthia and Adrianna, you made this book a reality.

Introduction

C ongratulations! You have just discovered a gold mine of proven strategies and applications to become a better leader. Inside you'll learn strategies that will show you how to communicate more effectively by developing your listening skills (which most people lack), techniques on how to find strength and peace in the silence, and so much more. *I don't want you to read this book.* I want you to **study it, apply,** and **talk about it** with your friends. Our retention of a concept is much greater when we apply it as opposed to just reading it. In doing so, you may discover this to be one of your favorite leadership books.

Put the material to practice. Don't be that person who buys a book and doesn't apply it.

Knowledge is not power; applied knowledge is power.

And you now hold in your hands the knowledge to take your leadership to the next level.

We hear the term "leadership" a lot—on the news, while watching our favorite sports team, and at work. It is one of the most commonly used—misused—words, and it can take on several definitions. What is your definition of *leadership?*

This book is my definition.

Leadership by Choice means making a conscious choice to positively influence those around you by managing yourself and leading others in four areas: communication, leading teams, productivity, and personal development.

We see leadership, or the lack of it, throughout our entire day. How effective are you in the following scenarios?

- Communication: Listening to a client and asking good open-ended questions and finding out how your service/product can be of value.
- Leading teams: Having clients believe you have their best interests in mind.
- Productivity: Developing a focused work approach that others admire and follow.
- Personal development: Supporting the ambitions/goals of office colleagues.

Leadership by Choice is full of applicable ideas and tips; you will also be entertained with true stories and impactful (sometimes humorous) illustrations. I kept the fluff in my marshmallow sandwiches and left my leadership theories with my college professors. This book is all about teaching you how to become a better leader using proven techniques.

Leadership Tip

A title in today's result-driven society is nothing more than ink on a business card. It's nice to have but bears little meaning. Leadership is not about what title or position you hold but rather a choice on how you lead. Would people still follow you regardless of your title or rank?

Leadership makes the difference every time on any level in any industry.

- It was Lincoln's leadership in the area of personal development that allowed him to keep his calm in uncertain times and lead us to a better America.
- It was Steve Jobs's leadership in the area of productivity that made our lives easier in the areas of cell phones, music, computers, purchasing, and more.
- It was George Steinbrenner's leadership in the area of leading teams that transformed a once-ailing team into the most dominant team in all of major league sports.
- It was Ronald Regan's leadership in the area of communication that garnered him the label as "the great communicator."

By trade I am a communicator. And I've had the privilege of meeting everyone from C-level executives to frontline employees. And I am a believer in that everyone has a story, a gift, and can teach us something. I've had the honor of teaching leadership and learning daily from everyone I encounter. *Leadership by Choice* is full of my best ideas and practical tips that I've accumulated over the years traveling the country and conducting management seminars.

This book is divided into four parts, each of which are areas where we can apply our leadership skills daily:

- **Part 1: Communication**—How well do you listen, ask questions, and speak with influence? How many of our problems are caused by lack of listening? In this section I tell the story of Leitha Lewis, an effective listener, and how you can improve your listening ability. You'll discover that many situations can be resolved by closing our mouths, listening, and asking questions. This section also contains practical tips for public speaking.

- **Part 2: Leading Teams**—How well do you establish trust, healthy conflict, and achieve results with others? One of the best advantages in any organization is developing leaders whom people will follow because they want to. In this section I give the instructions for building a successful foundation when establishing a team. This section also gives tips on how to hold people accountable and provides answers on how to deal with the Entitlement Generation: the next generation of leaders.
- **Part 3: Productivity**—How well do you spend your time, and how focused are you? There is a difference in activity and productivity. Hard work doesn't guarantee success anymore. In this section you'll discover the importance of knowing your priorities and what the power of focus can do for you.
- **Part 4: Personal Development**—What are you doing to develop yourself? Nothing is constant, not the stock market, the weather, our health, or our bank account. We are either making progress toward our goals or not. In this section you'll discover the key ingredient to accomplishing your goals and the importance of the silence.

Leadership by Choice is about making a conscious effort to become an effective leader in both your professional life and personal life. It's now time to study, apply, and talk about leadership.

PART
1

Communication

1 | Listen Like Leitha

At the University of Notre Dame, I had the pleasure of meeting Ms. Leitha Lewis, housekeeper of O'Neill Hall dormitory. She took the time to introduce herself and referred to us as her babies. When we first met, I thought this was just her way of introduction and didn't think anything of it, until I saw her days later.

She would greet each student with a smile—and not just any smile, a real smile. You know how some smiles look uncomfortable? Ms. Leitha's smile radiated sincerity and understanding, two very important traits of listening. She always listened to students, not with just an ear, but with both eyes, reflecting back their feelings. She also demonstrated other skills that made her a great listener.

After graduation and reflecting on what I had learned at Notre Dame, I discovered that the most powerful lesson came from her. Ms. Leitha taught me how to become an excellent listener, someone who could be "in the moment" when listening.

In this chapter, Ms. Leitha's name is an acronym for how to become a better listener:

L: Liking
E: Eyes, empathy, encouragement (oh my!)
I: "In the moment," "I am not the focus"
T: Time and take notes
H: Head and heart
A: Another time

Liking

Have you ever noticed when listening to someone that the more you like the person, the better listener you become? We listen better when we actually like the person; in fact, liking the person even makes it easier to remember that person's name and the conversation.

Do you remember the name of that cute guy or girl when you were growing up, the one who brought a smile to your face? For me, that girl was Brittany Dotson (hope she doesn't read this book!). Why do you remember a certain name? It's simple; because you like that person.

When you listen with liking, you give the person respect that says, "I want to understand you," and you make a deeper connection in your mind. Say your boss, whom you admire and respect, comes by your office to chat. Since you like him, it makes listening to him more natural.

What prevents us from listening with liking? Us! We sometimes have our own preconceived ideas and perceptions about someone. Sometimes while listening to someone, thoughts flood your mind—"Can this person do anything for me?" "I probably won't like this person," or "Who likes them anyway?"—influencing how you listen.

Nothing in this world is good or bad, but thinking makes it so.
—William Shakespeare

Listening with liking is much like cleaning a windshield. Your view of that person is open and not obstructed by something else. Listening with liking looks like a smile:

- Lean toward the person.
- Make eye contact with him or her.
- Reflect the other person's feelings without agreeing.
- Do your best to make the person feel comfortable.

Listen to someone you wouldn't normally talk to and discover what you can learn from him or her. Focus on similarities rather than differences.

Leadership Tip

When we like someone, we want to hear what that person has to say . . . and we seem to always find the time to listen.

Listening with Dislike

But what happens if you don't like the person? Have you ever experienced any of these scenarios?

1. You didn't care for your neighbor at first; then one day you actually became friends.
2. You met someone and were indifferent, but then over time you became that person's friend.
3. You couldn't stand your boss, until she opened up to you and you discovered she is a caring person.

Let's say you get a call one evening. When the person on the other end says he is from the IRS, your stomach starts to turn, sweat starts running down your brow, and your blood pressure goes up. Maybe you're nervous because you just heard a horror story involving a colleague at work about her encounter with the IRS and how it ended.

Before the person can ask a question, your mood turns to dislike, your tone becomes gruff, and your mind gets defensive and your answers short.

Stop a minute. Can you guess the outcome of the conversation? What tone will you convey to the caller? How quickly will listening with dislike resolve your tax issue? In your present state, you may find yourself in some type of confrontation.

If you remember one thing that I tell you, I hope it's that your behavior is a choice. When you feel yourself behaving a way you don't want to, pause and change it.

Eyes, Empathy, Encouragement (Oh My!)

The eyes are vital to listening, because you see facial expressions and body posture when you communicate. Also, when you make eye contact with someone, you demonstrate your focus on that person.

Not only did Ms. Leitha listen with liking, she also listened with her eyes. It's as if she used them as a mirror to reflect the other person's feelings. If you came in and were upset about a grade, her eyes reflected it. If you were excited with good news, so was she.

Has this ever happened to you? Someone enters your office, and your head is buried in the computer. You're checking e-mails or typing. You glance up very quickly and then glance back at your keyboard, and as you look back at the keyboard you say, "Go ahead, I'm listening," as you pound away furiously on the keys.

Does the message you send to that person really indicate that you're listening? No, because you're not making eye contact.

Do you ever wonder if people are listening to you, if they are truly excited to see you? Would you like to find out? One way is called the "eyebrow test." The next time you greet someone, watch the eyebrows. If they go up, that person is happy to see you.

Put the eyebrow test to use. When you're greeted by relatives at the next holiday gathering, watch their eyebrows when they answer the door. If you're greeted by a warm "It's so good to see you" and their eyebrows go up, it's a good sign, because it means they are generally interested in you.

The most important thing in communication is to hear what isn't being said.

—Peter Drucker

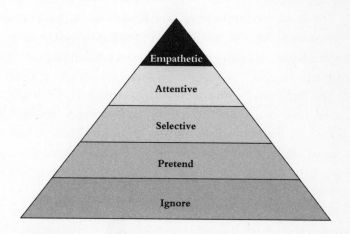

Referencing a Dale Carnegie instructor, the five levels of listening are:

1. Empathetic
2. Attentive
3. Selective
4. Pretend
5. Ignore

The first and highest level of listening is **empathetic.** Empathy is demonstrating that you are aware of others' thoughts and feelings and trying to understand them. To listen with empathy usually involves you asking a lot of questions to really understand someone or something.

The next level is **attentive**. At this point, you are paying attention and maybe able to memorize and repeat back what was said. An example is a student who gets a good grade on a test. But just because she gets a high grade doesn't mean she understands the material.

The third level is **selective** listening: hearing what you want to hear. For example, a wife tells her husband, "Go to the store, fix the door, organize your office, and you can watch the game." What the husband hears is, "I can watch the game."

The fourth level is **pretend**. This level of listening is common at networking functions and parties. Someone pretends to listen to someone he or she doesn't know, only to be searching for someone else to talk to.

The fifth level is **ignore**. We all have probably been guilty, at some time or another, of completely ignoring someone who is talking. A friend of mine named Chris learned how to ignore his mom while he was growing up. One day she needed a ride to work. Chris, listening on the lowest level, completely forgot, resulting in his mom having to walk three miles to work.

You have probably heard the expression, "to walk a mile in someone else's shoes." In other words, you get a feeling for what it's like in another person's situation, a concept related directly to listening. When listening to someone, look at that person's shoes to help you remember this point.

When we fail to picture ourselves in other people's shoes, often we "advice dump." We just dump our advice on them about what they need or should do, or question them without trying to fully understand their position. Remember, "their shoes" will help you empathize with them.

Do you remember your middle school days? Did you ever get into trouble? I once did something that landed me in the principal's office. I remember it still because the entire time I was talking to Sister Irene, it felt like she was casting judgment on me and not listening to my side of the story.

Have you ever felt that someone was judging you while you were talking? It's not a comfortable situation. People can tell if you are listening to them or judging them in a matter of minutes. Leave judgment to the courts, and do your best to understand the person you are engaged in conversation with by giving your full attention.

Here is an example of how understanding history can help us all become better listeners:

"The Kennedys stayed here. Matter of fact, a lot of famous people have stayed at this hotel," Paul, the bellhop at the Radisson in Lackawanna, Pennsylvania, said as he took my luggage to my room.

I was fascinated at how much Paul knew about the hotel. There was an obvious history about the place, and learning it gave me more of an appreciation of the building. As Paul continued, I thought of how this example relates to us all.

I've always been a fan of history, respectful of people who have gone before and paved the way in our own country, as well as in just about every industry and city.

How well do you know the history of your company? Do you know the pioneers in your profession or who had your job before you? Have you ever listened to their stories?

History teaches much on many levels. By understanding and appreciating the past, we can better connect to the present and the future. Knowledge of the past fosters clarity that allows us to focus on the future, and in this cyclic process our ability to listen is enhanced.

Encouragement

Encouragement enters our conversations, sometimes with great impact.

I was running on the track at the gym one day when I saw a young girl who was overweight and making an effort to get in shape by walking "It's good that you're walking," I said to her.

"What?" she asked, as she pulled her iPod from her ears.

"It's good that you're walking; keep it going," I repeated as I passed by her.

A sort of confused, happy look came over her face and then she replied, "Oh, thanks."

I finished my run and then began walking to cool down. I suddenly wondered, "What happened to my new friend?"

Looking around, I saw that she wasn't walking anymore; she was now running and almost out of sight. It was a struggle for her, but she persisted. I felt a huge grin creep across my face; she had made my day. Some days I go to the gym and lift heavier weights simply because I'm influenced by the atmosphere and encouragement of someone else there.

You may never know the impact of your words, but you can offer encouragement to others, including total strangers. Encouragement builds people up and empowers them, so be bold and start encouraging people today.

Leadership Tip

There are two types of people in this world; those who push you up and those who hold you down.

"In the Moment," "I Am Not the Focus"

Most people are not good listeners because they aren't fully present in the moment. Physically they are there, but their minds wander. For example, during a meeting, they might be thinking: "What time is this meeting going to end?" "I wonder what's for dinner tonight." "I wonder what's on television." "Oh, that's right; I've got to pick up my dry cleaning today."

They don't pay attention to the presenter, because they are not in the moment. When you listen to someone, make sure you are in the moment both physically and mentally.

Well-timed silence hath more eloquence than speech.

—Anonymous

I once worked as a personal trainer in a gym. It was a great experience to help people achieve their fitness goals, which came about by listening to the clients and understanding their current condition, setting goals, and deciding what type of plan was best for them.

C.J., a nice guy who made himself presentable and cared about people, was another trainer at the gym, but he wasn't very busy. I didn't know why at first, until one day while talking to him, it occurred to me that he wasn't successful because he didn't know how to listen. The conversation was always about him.

Any time you told him a story, as soon as you finished, he immediately told you another story on the same subject. It usually started with, "Oh yeah, well let me tell you about...," "That was nothing; one time...," "Wait till you hear this..."—like he never cared about what you said.

It was annoying at first, and soon you didn't want to talk to him. It was almost like he was playing the one-up game. Whatever you told him didn't matter; he had a story that was one better.

Do you ever catch yourself trying to one-up someone? Have you ever had a one-up game pulled on you? How does it make you feel?

When listening to someone, say to yourself, "I am not the focus." When listening to someone else's story, ask questions and comment on it. Don't launch into your own story.

We talk little if we do not talk about ourselves.

—William Hazlitt

Egoitis

Imagine you are speaking in a meeting and everyone is paying attention except your boss. So you think to yourself, "What gives? Why isn't he listening to me?"

Your boss could be suffering from *egoitis*. Although I made it up, this egotistic, self-centered concept has been around for many years. Egoitis blocks your ears and prevents you from listening to anyone below you on the corporate/social ladder.

Often the best ideas come from people on the front lines, not just those in the boardroom. It is important to remove the egoitis and listen to people on all levels rather than be blinded by their titles or positions.

Eliminate the "I" in biographical listening. An example of "I am not the focus" is biographical listening after talking to someone who tells you what he or she did. For example, a kid comes home from school and is upset about a bad test grade he received. His parents are paying big bucks to send him to this private school, and at the dinner table he is greeted by his father asking, "How was your day, son?"

"Fine," he replies.

Detecting something is wrong, Dad starts to investigate. "What's the matter, son?"

"I got a bad score on my math test."

The boy opens up and begins the dialogue, and then Dad goes into "I" mode. "What do you mean you got a bad grade? When *I* was your age, *I* was good in math. *I* would have studied harder. *I* was a good student. *I* had to work, and *I* even played football. *I* just don't understand how you can get a bad grade."

Does this sound familiar? Does this make the boy want to open up and share more or talk about his issues? Probably not. So as much as possible, avoid the "I" approach in conversations.

Calling People by Name

Knowing someone's name is important and can be beneficial in most situations. As I purchased a book one evening, I was greeted at the counter by a 19-year-old cashier. I was within seven inches of laying down my book when I quickly glanced at his name tag and said, "Hey Jack, how ya doing?"

Jack, the cashier at the local bookstore, grew two inches taller as he stood proudly ready to take my order. Then he did something out of the ordinary. He asked, "Sir, would you like 25 percent off your purchase today?"

I quickly responded, "Absolutely!"

Jack reached below the counter and scanned a coupon for my purchase, and I thought to myself: "What caused Jack to ask me that? Was there a system for that? Did he do it to every third customer? Did he do it for all the customers?"

We engaged in small talk, and then Jack delivered the line of the night. He looked at me like we had been friends since kindergarten and said, "Have a great night, Eric."

What the . . . ? How did he know my name? Ah, he must have looked at my debit card while we were talking. I thought to myself, "Good one, Captain Jack, you've got the importance of knowing a name down pat, and that principle will serve you well in business and in life."

When I called him by his name, I recognized him and made him my focus, which prompted him to memorize mine and call me by my name.

In a society full of texting, e-mails, BlackBerrys, and crackberries, how quickly we lose sight of calling people by their name. Call people by their name and you put the focus on them by silently saying, "You matter."

The sweetest sound to a person's ears is their own name.
—Dale Carnegie

When I gave public seminars, I had an audience of anywhere between 40 and 80 people. I would make it a point to memorize and say all their names within the first 10 minutes of my introduction. People were stunned and didn't know what to think—until I explained the importance of knowing someone's name. We remember what's important to us.

The next time you buy gas or groceries, call someone by his or her name and put the focus on that person. When you talk to someone, make the conversation about him or her. Ask more questions, close your mouth, and open your ears and eyes. See if you can listen 80 percent and talk 20 percent during the conversation.

Time and Take Notes

Many of us are rushed these days, either coming from a place but don't know where we were or running to a place but don't know where we're going. We have so many distractions, and sometimes it can cause us to forget something when we are listening.

A great tool to help us is a notepad. When you're engaged in a conversation, just write down notes on a notepad. Having a notepad handy demonstrates that you are willing to go the extra mile when listening and not relying solely on your memory. Taking notes demonstrates a higher level of listening and your actions say "What you say is important and I don't want to forget it."

People don't care how much you know until they know how much you care.

—Anonymous

Head and Heart

It is important that as a leader you listen with your head and your heart. It is essential that you understand what is on people's minds and in their hearts. Great leaders able to do this were Abraham Lincoln, Mahatma Gandhi, Mother Teresa, Dr. Martin Luther King, Jr., and many others.

Listening with just your head can make you appear cold and immune to someone's feelings. Listening with just your heart you risk becoming emotionally hijacked, where your emotions get the best of you and you tear up in the conversation or have an emotional outburst.

I fly all over the country giving speeches and doing training and naturally, I spend time on airplanes. Southwest Airlines is an airline I've noticed that listens both with the head and the heart. They do a great job of appealing to what's on a customer's mind (money) and listening with their heart (service).

You can tell when a company listens to and likes their customers by their happy employees, always calm and cheerful. By listening to their customers, they know that price and service are important, so they keep costs down and services high.

Another Time

We've talked about what it takes to become a great listener, now let's see what happens when you apply it. The real test of whether or not you have succeeded in becoming a great listener is if people return to you for future advice or counsel.

Ed Mack is the rector at O'Neill Hall and knows Ms. Leitha Lewis. He is also a great listener. As rector of the hall, he serves as the father figure for 275 young men in the dormitory. Ed is the type of listener that, when the conversation is over, you want to start a new one.

Do you know anyone who inspires you to come back another time, someone in your office who might be the "office shrink"? How do you claim that skill? People with that quality usually have good memories of their conversations with you, and having a good memory of the conversation will make people want to come back to converse with you.

My formula for having a great memory and bringing people back to you is DAC: *d*esire, *a*ttention, and *c*oncentration.

When something is important to you, your desire goes up, and when desire is high, memory is high:

$$\uparrow \text{Desire} = \uparrow \text{Memory}$$

When desire is high, you begin to focus and your attention grows, and when you are attentive, your concentration improves. These progressive steps promote better listening skills, because you actually focus on what someone is saying.

Six Pitfalls to Avoid

1. **"I know what you're going to say."** Being familiar with someone, we assume we know what that person will say and often miss much of what is actually said.

2. **"Here's what I would do."** We advice dump, giving solutions rather than understanding the content of what is said.

3. **"Talking is cool in our society."** Being a professional speaker is cool, but no one becomes a professional listener. In school we spend hours learning to read and write, to speak and communicate effectively, but we never learn how to listen properly.

4. **"Can you do anything for me?"** In our society, we sometimes don't listen to someone if they can't do something for us.

5. **"Just text it to me."** We have short attention spans and are constantly distracted.

6. **"We have bad models."** Maybe we grew up in a household where nobody listened and everyone was a "Chatty Cathy."

If listening to another person is an art, become an artist.

—Anonymous

2

Speaking with Influence

The Power of Speech

In 2004 at the Democratic National Convention in Boston, Massachusetts, John Kerry and John Edwards were running for president and vice president of the United States of America. Illinois US Senate candidate and keynote speaker, Barack Obama, gave an electrifying speech that not only put him on the map but put him in the minds of many Americans. In 2009 he became the US president.

During his inaugural address in January 1961, President John F. Kennedy said these famous words: "Ask not what your country can do for you—ask what you can do for your country." They inspired and influenced millions of people to take action. Powerful speakers influence people with their words, whether speaking one on one or to crowds numbering in the thousands.

The Audience and You

A speaker should apply certain universal points of speech, whether giving a keynote speech or talking to people in a meeting. These points are connect, hope, and inform.

The first point is to **connect**. As the speaker, you want to connect with your audience so that they feel like they understand you and almost know you. Whenever possible, get to know your audience before your speech begins. Also work on yourself, because the more authentic you are and the more you believe in your message, the easier it is to connect with your audience.

When I gave public seminars, I first met with everyone and called them by their name. By memorizing their names, the audience and I had already established a connection.

The second point is **hope**. I believe that all speakers want to give hope to their audiences. Today, we live in a world where doom and gloom seem to exist, and as a speaker you must be a conveyer of hope, encouraging people and lifting them up, whether giving quarterly results or a project status report. After all, the promise of hope and change won Barack Obama the US presidential election in 2008.

The third point is to **inform**. One way to do this is to raise the audience's level of awareness of a particular subject or cause. Another way is to teach them a valuable lesson by sharing a particular story or sharing a concept that can help them in some capacity.

Influence through Stories

The ability to tell stories is powerful because we remember stories. We relate to stories because they connect points. People may not remember your point, but they will remember your story. And if they remember your story, they can remember your point.

Relive your story so that your audience sees it. Bring your emotions, your character, and your feelings into the picture. The more you can relive your story, the stronger the impact is for your audience.

Focus on the *you* language. Instead of saying, "I did this, and I did that," relive your story and take the audience with you as though you're inviting them: "Come along with me . . .," "Imagine you are . . ."

And remember to add props to your story to prove your point or to add emphasis to a specific point.

The Power of Visualization

When I began my speaking career, I'd go into the meeting room, usually the night before, put a chair center stage, sit down, and visualize my speech for the next day. I'd visualize people nodding and laughing during my speech and people shaking my hand at the end of the seminar, saying, "Great seminar. I loved it. It's one of the best I've ever attended."

My speaking visualizations normally took about 20 minutes, and I believe they helped expedite my career and make me successful as a speaker. I was asked to compete in a toastmaster contest as an evaluator. I was judged on my evaluation of a speaker. I won my club, then the area, and then the region. And at the state tournament, 10 other contestants and I presented evaluations on the same speaker before 300 people.

Arriving the night before, I followed my usual routine. I took a chair, sat center stage, and mentally did the evaluation with my eyes closed, as if giving a real evaluation and speech. With great success, I took third place overall and was very pleased with my performance. To this day I still visualize my speeches.

A Speech Outline

Follow an outline that contains your desired outcome, the content for your audience, and the makeup of your audience.

What is your desired outcome? What do you want your audience members to do? Do you want to inform them or have them take action on something? Do you want to transfer a skill or knowledge, bring something to their attention, or raise their level of awareness on a particular issue?

Decide these issues before you give your speech. What is the content for your audience? What content do you want to stress? Do you want to cover 10 bullet points in 60 minutes or 8 bullet points in 30 minutes? I suggest that less is more. Instead of cramming in five bullet points, focus on three using stories, examples, and props that reinforce so that people know exactly what you talked about.

Who is your audience? Evaluate your audience beforehand for the best topic. Two of my clients are the National Association of

Catering Executives and the Utility Supply Management Alliance. The manner in which I present to the catering executives is different than my talk for the other group.

Also realize the time of day that you give your speech and consider many aspects. Is it while people are eating lunch or an after-dinner speech where cocktails are being served?

Are You Nervous?

Always remember that no matter how many speeches you give or how many presentations or meetings you conduct, you will always have some form of anxiety. But you should embrace that anxiety and realize that this is a form of excitement and not something to shy away from.

Realize that what is going on inside of you is much worse than what the audience experiences. If you are standing behind a podium and feel your knees start to shake a little (which mine have!), realize that the audience will not see that.

And don't tell the audience, "I'm nervous." When you start off with, "Please excuse me, I'm nervous," it just draws attention to your nervousness. If you tell them, then they think, "Oh man, looks like this is going to be a real dull speech."

Don't even worry about that. Realize that your nerves exist and embrace them, but focus on your message and the outcome that you want.

Leadership Tip

Pressure is life letting us know that we are alive. Learn to embrace it by staying focused on your purpose.

Crap Detector

We've all heard someone speak and start to sense that something isn't right. Bells are going off in our head; whistles are blowing—our alarm is sounding. I like to call that our "crap detector." Our crap detector goes off to let us know, "This person's full of it."

To avoid someone's crap detector going off during your speech, make sure that you believe in what you're saying, because your audience can see it when you don't. They can see it in your eyes, in your movements, in your passion, and in your tone of voice.

Power of the Pause

Pausing allows for reflection and mental digestion. Sometimes speakers just want to talk and talk, figuring that the more they talk, the more the audience will understand. But that's incorrect. In your presentations, pause and allow people to mentally digest what you're saying. Let it all sink in so that everyone processes all of your information and understands it.

Tennis and Audience Awareness

Being aware of your audience is like playing tennis. Tennis is a back-and-forth sport played with two players on a court. They each use a racket and hit a ball over a net. It goes back and forth, and sometimes long volleys take place. Similar to tennis, the speaker is on one side of the net and the audience on the other side.

Periodically, you need to be sure that when you send a point, talk about something, or tell a story or a funny joke that your audience receives it. The audience's facial expressions, laughter, or frowns tell you if they received it. If they get it, they smile or their eyes light up, and they send the "ball" back.

The ability to read your audience is a great indicator of when you need to speed up or slow down or when you need to repeat something because they didn't understand it. If you see confusion on the faces of your audience, you might need to take a break and clarify your message.

Distractions

Distractions are prevalent today, especially with the importance placed on e-mails and text messages. Some audience members will likely use their cell phones during your speech, but realize that distractions happen and don't take it personally. Your focus and commitment is to be responsible for delivering your message. Ultimately, the audience is responsible for their actions of whether or not they act on your message.

You Are the Message

Whether giving a keynote speech, speaking at a Parent-Teachers Association (PTA) meeting, your church, or a conference, you are the message. People notice how you dress, how you behave on and off stage, and if you are authentic. How well you connect with the audience is important. The more authentic you are, the deeper your connection with the audience will be. The deeper the connection you have, the more impact your message carries.

You are your message 24/7. The way you dress and carry yourself evolves into how well you can speak with influence. Your audience knows you as a speaker, but they also take everything they know about you into account, whether it's something they've personally read, heard, or seen about you or whether it comes from someone else.

Leadership Tip

People will buy into you first, before they buy into your message. So make sure you and your message are one.

Eye Contact

Making eye contact is important when speaking. Have you ever seen a speaker who makes eye contact with the ceiling, the walls, the floor, but never with anyone in the audience? Most people find it distracting. It takes away from the message.

Always make eye contact with someone in your audience when giving a speech. Lock eyes with someone for 3 or 4 seconds and then move to someone else. It's like talking one on one, when it's really maybe 1 on 30, but your audience feels as if you're actually talking to an individual.

The Ring Twirl and Side to Side

Have you ever seen speakers play with their rings, move from side to side, or move in some other way that is distracting? Have you watched as they take their hands out of their pockets and put them back in, only to take them out again? Do some of them look like they just figured out they have hands and are trying to figure out what to do with them?

Movements can be distracting to an audience. A great way to control this is to stand firm as you begin your presentation and move only with purpose, for example, to show a point or to bring the audience to another level. Stay focused. Don't move just for the sake of moving around.

Dealing with Difficulties

Effective leaders deal with touchy subjects and difficult conversations by addressing the issue head-on. If not addressed immediately, it can quickly become a problem. In such situations, it's important for speakers to watch their tone of voice and to keep it in, what I like to call, a "pass the salt" tone, as if in a restaurant conversation with someone while sharing a meal.

Humor Helps

Aspiring speakers sometimes ask, "Do I need to be humorous in order to be a professional speaker?" The answer usually is, "Only if you want to get paid."

I've seen economists, people who talk about sexual violence, and others who speak on an array of subjects successfully implement humor. Self-deprecating humor is one of the best ways to incorporate humor into your talks. I usually find it to be very acceptable and make fun of myself often.

People want to laugh and enjoy the moment. You want to speak with influence so that people understand your content. But at the same time, people want to relax, enjoy the experience, and have fun. Entertaining your audience with humor is a big element of influence.

A sense of humor is a sign of intelligence.

Be Human

Everyone makes mistakes, and when you make a mistake, say two words to yourself: "So what?" Allow for mistakes and keep going. People make mistakes all the time. Just turn on the TV to watch someone on the late show, a news anchor, or a politician being interviewed and you'll see proof.

Even a famous comedian like Jay Leno on *The Tonight Show* makes mistakes. And what happens? He just keeps going. If you come off too scripted or appearing too flawless, people sometimes question whether or not you are genuine or authentic.

The Gettysburg Address

You're probably familiar with Abraham Lincoln's Gettysburg Address. It was only 272 words. Lincoln wasn't even the featured speaker for the event. Edward Everett was the featured speaker who got up and spoke for about two hours. You might not have known that Edward Everett was the featured speaker at the event, but you probably knew that Lincoln delivered the Gettysburg address.

Less is more. Don't say something in 20 minutes that can be said in 2. Think of the impact Lincoln's 272-word Gettysburg Address contained, versus Edward Everett's nearly two-hour oration. It's a matter of quality, not quantity.

Four Steps to Successful Speaking

Before I tell you my four-step process to successful speaking, let me share a story of panic. I was asked to speak at a luncheon where the audience consisted of influential businesspeople and community leaders. While seated at a table, the waiter began serving the salads. I generally don't eat at events before I speak, but I was especially hungry that day.

I figured I'd quickly eat a light salad. I was only on my second bite when the person who booked me stood up and started to read my introduction. I had thought I was going to speak after lunch, but it looked like it was showtime.

I'm not fond of speaking to groups during lunch or after dinner, because it can sometimes be tough to keep their attention. But I got up and began my speech.

I had been caught a bit off guard but soon began to settle down into my material. Lunch continued, and the waiter reappeared and started to serve the main entrée—and walked right in front of me as he did so. My audience's attention was now consumed with the thought of their chicken parmesan. At this point, I was frustrated and felt like I was the background music at an upscale restaurant.

A part of me wanted to walk out, but I knew if I walked out or stopped to ask, "Are you listening?" that I was putting the audience in control of the situation. That's when I decided I was going to get through the speech, no matter what, and focus my attention on the people listening to me. And I did.

I discovered that when your audience upsets you, they control you. Speakers must remember their commitment to an audience, even if the audience didn't make a commitment to listen.

You tell the world who you are when you speak, and in doing so, you must offer something of value. I've devised an acronym for a strategy known as PVAR: prepare, visualize, act, and review. If you follow these four simple strategies, I guarantee your chances for success will increase.

Prepare

Preparation
Begets
Confidence

You must prepare to achieve success in any aspect of life, especially when speaking to an audience and making your point. A speaking opportunity is worth exactly what your preparation allows you to make of it. You connect with your audience only if you believe your product or service can render value to them. Why speak to them if you have nothing prepared and insightful to˜say?

Preparation is important, especially in your first speech. First impressions can have an impact on whether or not you are asked to speak again, so be prepared.

As an Eagle Scout in the Boy Scouts of America, I heard two words routinely: "Be prepared" (the Boy Scouts' motto). Being prepared in the speaking industry means preparing for as much as you can control.

Be prepared about what you wear, maybe wearing a favorite suit or tie, and make sure that you feel great during your presentation. Have a checklist of prepared notes and handouts and always have extras on hand. Your audience assumes that you are the authority figure. If you are the least bit uncertain about your material, it will show.

Prepare for technology failures and for rude guests and hecklers in the audience and know how to deal with them. Make sure you are prepared for tough questions. Some audience members may challenge your topic, so be ready for it. Be prepared and expect the best, but prepare for the worst.

Visualize

Visualizing the outcome of a situation helps you achieve a desired result. I tested this strategy in high school. After two knee surgeries and not being able to play football my senior year, I decided to throw the discus. We didn't have a discus coach, so I taught myself by going to the library 20 minutes a day and watching videos of collegiate and Olympic athletes repeatedly throwing the discus.

On some occasions, I visualized myself making a perfect throw just liked I studied from the computer throwing a perfect throw. I burned an image in my head of what a perfect throw looked like, and when I got to practice, I brought out that image. Ultimately, I was runner-up in the state of Florida for discus.

Watch successful speakers and learn from them. Watch how they use their hand gestures and listen to how they change their voice. Watch television preachers. Mute the volume and focus on how they move their bodies.

Next, see yourself giving an awesome speech and people immediately jumping to their feet to give you a standing ovation. See people approach you wanting to shake your hand. Hear the compliments you will receive after your speech.

A key component in visualization is to know the room where you will present. As previously stated, I spend about 20 minutes imagining the people in the audience, and then I walk around the room and act out my speech.

Most people fail to visualize the moments leading up to the victory. It's easy to visualize everyone in the audience on their feet and applauding, but what about just before you take the stage? What do you feel then?

If you want to become a successful speaker, you must visualize the pressure and learn to embrace it. Anyone who is very successful in his or her profession is very good under pressure. These people view pressure as a challenge and love it. Being able to visualize the pressure and see yourself overcome it ultimately leads to a successful speech.

Act

Once you have prepared and visualized the desired outcome, have fun. This is the best part of the experience, because it's what you have so diligently worked toward. It's like losing a lot of weight, and now it's time to buy a new pair of jeans and reveal yourself.

Will you be nervous before you speak? Probably, but so what? Remember, you are prepared and ready for the speech. Preparation stimulates confidence, and confidence builds a successful speaker.

Your audience will know in the first 10 minutes if you are confident and know your topic. Often, the audience is looking to see if you believe what you are saying. When they see that you believe it, they will continue to listen.

Remember to smile when you give a speech. Smiling is contagious. Popular preacher Joel Osteen does this all the time. Smiling puts the audience at ease and shows that you enjoy what you do, especially when you make it look so natural.

If you mess up, remember these two words: "So what?" Making a mistake shows your audience that you are human. I've found that when speakers are too smooth, they come off as canned or scripted, and I find myself thinking I could have just watched their video.

If you make a mistake and forget to say a word, just keep going. When you take time out and acknowledge your mistake, it takes away from your message.

Remember, obstacles are what you see when you take your eyes off the objective. Your objective is to give value to your audience and to enjoy giving the speech.

Review

Speaking is a process, and immediately following my speeches I do a mental review and ask myself two questions: "How did I do?" and "How can I get better?" The first is based on your standards, no one else's. The next question is about how you can make it better.

I operate with the philosophy that I have yet to give a perfect speech. The day I give a perfect speech is the day I start another profession.

Another way to review is to get feedback. Hand out evaluation forms containing three to four simple questions to your audience and the person who hired you to make sure you met their objectives.

If you really want to be the best, hire a speaking coach. Have someone you know and trust provide you with truthful feedback. Have direct connection with your coach, someone who will genuinely believe in you and knows what it takes to succeed. A wise man, Ben Johnson, once said: "To speak and to speak well are two things. A fool may talk, but a wise man speaks."

3

The Importance of Questions

Don't Answer Your Own Questions

Growing up, my dad taught me the value of questions and always told me not to answer my own questions. Often he would say, "We all have questions, and we hurt ourselves by answering our own questions."

For example, say you're at a clothing store and you notice that a pair of jeans has two prices, $89.99 and a $29.99 reduced price. You look at both and think, "It can't possibly be $30 for this pair of jeans."

Without hesitation or asking a store clerk, you walk away without actually knowing the real answer. Maybe that's the price and maybe not, but you gain no information at all by answering your own question.

I always wanted to attend the University of Notre Dame, but I knew that it would be too academically competitive to go there right out of high school. Most people at this point would stop and think, "If I can't get in my freshman year, I'll just go somewhere else." But I didn't do that.

My question was, Could I transfer there and, if so, what was that process? Rather than asking and answering my own questions, I did the research and found out that, yes, I could transfer and learned about those requirements. After completing my freshman year at the University of South Florida, I applied and was accepted into the University of Notre Dame.

Leaders ask good questions and then sit back and listen. They don't pretend to know all the answers.

Questions and Onions

At some point, you have probably asked a question and received half an answer or very little response. If you have ever cut an onion in half, you've probably noticed that it has layers. Asking questions is similar to an onion, in that you need to go deeper to get at the core of the matter.

For example, your spouse comes home from work and says, "I want to quit my job."

You ask, "Why do you want to quit your job?"

"Well, it's the commute. The commute is so long and takes about 45 minutes. It's very stressful in the morning."

"So you want to quit your job because of the commute?"

"Well, that's not exactly it. I'm getting paid very little, and I don't even know if it's making that much of a difference, in terms of the income I'm bringing in."

"So you want to quit your job because you feel like you're not getting paid enough?"

The conversation continues, and just like peeling an onion, you go deeper and deeper to get at the core of the issue. Ultimately, you discover that your spouse feels like quitting after having a very bad day and receiving very little recognition at work. But you had to go through several layers to get to that core point.

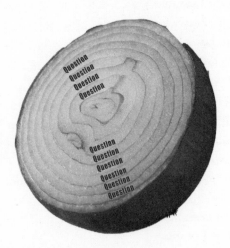

Questions and Assumptive Listening

Do you ever catch yourself saying, "I thought you meant . . . ," or, "I assumed you . . ."? As you've probably heard before, when you assume anything, it generally makes an "ass" out of "u" and "me."

I once flew home from a business trip and realized that I hadn't left a car at the airport for my return home. To help me out, my parents dropped off my car. In a phone conversation, my dad said, "I left the car in the long-term parking lot."

I thanked him and quickly hung up the phone, assuming he meant the economy parking lot.

After landing, I made my way to the off-site economy parking lot for people who want to leave their car for an extended period of time and looked for the car there. But after about a half-hour, I called my dad again; again he said "long-term."

"I thought you meant economy," I said.

But he replied no and I continued. "Oh, I just assumed that's what you meant."

I felt like an idiot and wasted a lot of time.

People often assume rather than ask more questions on a particular issue. For example, maybe in a meeting your boss says, "I want all projects on my desk by Friday," and you assume he wants all projects you're working on. But he might just want the one dealing with that meeting.

Assumptive listening is the result of assuming what someone else is actually saying. As much as possible, avoid being caught in assumptive listening by asking as many questions as may be necessary to sufficiently address and resolve your questions. No one enjoys feeling like an idiot.

Questions, Understanding, and Credibility

Asking questions demonstrates a desire to understand something. Three great types of questions to ask are

1. Clarifying questions
2. Paraphrasing questions
3. Follow-up questions

Clarifying questions are posed to better understand an issue or subject. For example:

- "What I heard you say was . . ."
- "If I understand you correctly . . ."
- "What does that mean?"
- "Can you share some examples?"
- "Can you be more specific?"
- "Can you clarify that for me?"

Paraphrasing questions simply restate what someone told you and demonstrate an improved level of understanding. For example:

- "So, what you're telling me is . . ."
- "X, Y, and Z are the most important to you, is that correct?"

Follow-up questions are posed to reach a solution, an agreement, or a type of commitment. For example:

- "As a result of our conversation . . ."
- "The next time we meet, would you like . . . ?"
- "What is the best way to follow up on . . . ?"

Asking any of these questions demonstrates that you have a genuine interest in trying to understand someone and that you are making a great attempt to listen to the other person.

Asking good questions also demonstrates your credibility as a listener:

1. It gets the other person talking. People like to hear themselves talk, and questions get others talking about themselves and what's important to them.
2. It demonstrates your ability to listen and shows that you don't think the air has to be filled just with your voice.
3. It gives you more of an understanding of and insight into their issues. By asking the right questions, you can then tailor your information to meet their needs.

Repeat Questions

Sometimes when I see a politician or a coach being interviewed on television, I notice that they go off track. A news reporter will ask a simple question, and the person interviewed gives some long-winded answer, but never really answers the question. I'm always interested to see if the reporter will ask the same question again, maybe in a slightly different way, or if he or she will simply go on to something else. If this happens to you, simply ask the question again, because the person may have forgotten your question. Don't be afraid to ask questions, and take notes.

Brevity is important in asking good questions, so keep your questions short. Don't ask more than one question at a time, or one filled with two or three questions within that question. It gives the person leeway to dissipate the original question and avoid answering altogether.

Open-Ended versus Closed-Ended Questions

There are two types of questions: open-ended questions and closed-ended questions. Examples of open-ended questions include:

- "Describe the . . ."
- "Tell me about the . . ."
- "What challenges . . . ?"
- "Why or how did you do . . . ?"

Asking open-ended question gets the person talking more easily and gives you a better understanding as to what's important to them. You gain more information from open-ended questions then close-ended questions. For example, "Did you and your previous boss get along?" If the reply is, "No," potentially valuable information is lacking that may be important to you, particularly in a hiring situation.

Asking open-ended questions gives people an opportunity to provide a more thorough answer. For example, "How would you describe the relationship with your boss?" is an open-ended question. There is no predetermined list of answers to this questions. An open-ended reply to this question might be, "He's the best boss I've ever had. He listens and takes my suggestions seriously."

Asking closed-ended questions often gets a basic yes or no answer, providing you with very limited information.

Think about the questions you ask your customers and prospective clients. Have a list of open-ended questions designed to give you more information and insight into what they do, think, and like. With a list you can better determine how to best pair your service, offer value, and help them with what you both want to accomplish.

It amazes me that when some people ask a question, they fail to allow adequate time for a response. They ask a question and almost immediately interrupt the attempt to answer, trying to answer the question themselves, asking another question, or becoming defensive.

Always allow the person you ask a question of to think about his or her reply, to mentally digest what you just asked, and to process the information. Don't be uncomfortable with the silence. If you ask someone a tough question on a tough subject, you might allow 10 to 30 seconds to pass so that the other person can reply properly and confidently.

People are usually more convinced by reasons they discover themselves than by those found by others.

—Blaise Pascal

Question Your Tone and Motive

People can tell when they are being interrogated, and they know when someone asks a question and already knows the answer, as seen on TV shows that involve a witness stand. The tone of the conversation takes on a totally different quality.

Be aware of your motive. If you ask a question, know the answer, and are trying to get someone to admit something, it can make for a very uncomfortable situation for both parties, especially if the other person becomes defensive.

When asking questions, be aware of how you pose them and the tone of your voice. Keep your tone level conversational and avoid using a tone that in any way sounds like interrogation, especially when your goal is to gain information and insight.

Curiosity Brings Innovation

Sometimes I babysit my three-year-old nephew. At one stage in his life he just kept asking, "Why?" After *everything* I said, he immediately asked why this or why that. I would answer, and he would respond with another "Why?" He would ask three to five times on any topic, and I was quickly losing my patience—until I realized his motive.

His motive wasn't to upset me, make me feel stressed, or annoy me. It was simple curiosity. He truly was curious and wanted to know more. He had taught me a valuable lesson, and for that I will always be appreciative.

Be careful of responding too quickly—and be especially careful of too quickly dismissing someone with a "Because I said so." Think how you would feel if you brought up an idea in your organization only to somebody quickly stomp on it with, "Well, that's the way we've always done it." Or if you asked a question about a topic of interest to you only to have it dismissed without consideration. Such responses negatively impact people's curiosity and creativity.

Asking relevant, well-thought-out questions promotes curiosity and innovation, but creativity suffers when someone makes a negative statement. Such a response frustrates the person asking the question and deters him or her from asking more questions and giving input. Also, that individual becomes more reluctant to engage further in the conversation.

Most often, asking good questions produces a better understanding of why someone does something a particular way, gives insight into his or her goals and motives, and illuminates a more efficient way of communicating and doing business.

PART

2 | Leading Teams

4

The Abdication
of Accountability

Sue You!

"Have your feelings been hurt today at work? Has somebody caused you distress? If so, call the law offices of 1-800-JoeNoResponsibility."

Some days you can't go 5 minutes without hearing an advertisement for some type of lawyer. We live in a society where people point the finger, not at themselves, but at others. "Hey, it's not my fault; I can just hire an attorney." "Hey, it's not my fault; it's my boss's fault."

This type of mentality permeates our culture, as seen in some reality TV shows. When it first came out, one of my favorite reality shows was *The Apprentice,* a show where people competed to be Donald Trump's next apprentice. Each week, someone not up to the task was fired from the show. But in later seasons, getting fired centered on drama in the boardroom and who could best defend himself or herself.

More and more frequently, "You're fired!" seemed to center around defending a lack of accountability. This meant that everyone focused on trying to pinpoint flaws in someone else's performance, for fear of being fired themselves.

That's the wrong lesson to teach people, because it teaches them that they can avert their responsibility by blaming others. And whoever is better at deflecting the blame is the winner, which hardly seems fair or worthy of admiration.

Unfortunately, in today's society we seem to hold people less and less accountable for their actions, and we are paying the price for it. When you breed and teach a culture of no accountability, it's very hard to reach anything above mediocrity.

Responsibility is the price of greatness.

—Winston Churchill

Good Employees, Punished; Bad Ones, Rewarded

Recently I ran into my friend, Doug, who looked distressed. When I asked what was wrong, he said that lately he had been dealing with a lot of stress at work with Mark, a man who works in his department and who had been with the company for a longer time than my friend had.

Every time Doug tried to hold Mark accountable, for example, by asking for something that was due or following up on a project, Mark would complain to someone higher up, saying that Doug was treating him unfairly. Then Doug would find himself not only in trouble with his boss but having to pick up Mark's slack as well.

This example indicates that good employees do get punished, like Doug, who is hardworking and trying to do his best. He gets punished and called into human resources (HR) while Mark gets off scot-free—all because Mark has been at the company longer and the company doesn't hold people accountable.

Unfortunately, this story is not uncommon in many organizations, where *good employees get punished by getting more work and more responsibility* while *bad employees are rewarded with more time to do a job and less responsibility.* A manager simply doesn't put a project on just anyone's plate. He gives it to someone he knows can get the job done even though that person might already have a lot of work.

Not holding people accountable in organizations is a big problem. If this mind-set exists in your organization, it needs to stop. The idea that someone can't be fired because he or she is in a protected class or union and because it will take an act of Congress to do so, creates a breeding ground for below-average performance. And until we hold people responsible for their actions, this type of behavior will continue and the results will be below average.

People think responsibility is hard to bear. It's not. I think that sometimes it is the absence of responsibility that is harder to bear. You have a great feeling of impotence.

—Henry Kissinger

Wall Street . . . No Accountability

I love America, which gives us many freedoms. But with freedom comes responsibility and accountability, both of which are lacking on Wall Street. The greed and pure selfish acts of several of Wall Street's influencers is what fueled our financial recession in 2008.

> *What profit would there be for one to gain the whole world and forfeit his life?*
>
> —The Bible, Matthew, Chapter 16:26

Watch the documentary *Inside Job*, and you'll get a financial picture that is disturbing and one that *must* change. The old motto, "Well, everyone else is doing it," is a response of a coward, not a leader.

Do you respect those who hold themselves accountable, or those who want money at any price? Whatever happened to earning an honest living?

Life's Problems

> *You must take personal responsibility. You cannot change the circumstances, the seasons, or the wind, but you can change yourself. That is something you have charge of.*
>
> —Jim Rohn

Do any of the following describe the major problem in your life?

"The problem of my life is that I don't get paid enough." "The problem of my life is I don't like my job." "The problem of my life is my boss is too hard on me." "The problem of my life is I live in a very cold climate and the weather stinks."

"The problem of my life is my car; it never runs correctly." "The problem of my life is my relationship with my wife; she's always upset." "The problem of my life is my kids, who never listen."

"The problem of my life is I'm out of shape and don't have the time to get back in shape." "The problem of my life is I don't have any money."

The problem of my life is I don't accept responsibility and I don't hold myself accountable. And when I start holding myself accountable, then my problems will start to go away.

Five Ways to Hold Yourself Accountable

1. **Don't overextend yourself.** So often people involve themselves in too many projects. They put their name in the hat or sign up for a new project, saying, "I'll be there at this certain time," and they find themselves overly committed. Don't take on more than you can handle.

2. **Take action before you speak.** Remember that actions speak louder than words. If your goal is to write a proposal, just start writing it and then tell people about it. Instead of just talking about it, actually jump in and do it.

3. **Have an accountability partner.** If you don't feel like taking your daily walk after your workday, when your neighbor knocks on the door at 6 PM, it's hard to answer, "I'm not going because I'm lazy tonight." Alone you might not do it, but if someone holds you accountable, chances are you'll grab your running shoes. Have an accountability partner for your personal and professional goals.

4. **Chart your progress.** When you can actually see your progress, your confidence increases. Have a small notepad or a dry erase board to write down daily or weekly actions that chart your continual growth.

5. **Aim for consistency, not perfection.** Being consistent enables you to create a habit of starting something and holding yourself accountable as you continue to develop self-discipline.

Tenure Equals No Accountability

I'm often amazed when I hear teachers talk about tenure, whether at the college or high school level. It's a very disturbing concept, because tenure means a lack of accountability—or very loose efforts in terms of accountability.

People get upset when their comfort zone is threatened and they worry about being fired. If we want our school systems to improve, we must start with our leaders in the classroom. How can teachers hold their students accountable if they are not willing to hold themselves to higher standards?

Tenure can breed weak leadership and poor results, low standards and lack of accountability, and an environment where good gets punished and bad gets rewarded.

Most teachers are amazing people, and many influential people in my life were either teachers or coaches. They get paid very little and put up with so much. Both of my parents were in education.

A teacher for 33 years, my mom taught in a private Catholic school, where each year she was evaluated on performance, not experience. If she did well, she kept her job and her annual contract was renewed. By holding teachers to a higher standard, where teachers were held accountable and, in turn, held their students accountable, the school was one of the best, with a waiting list to get in.

We need to wake up and provide better leadership in our schools and communities, but it starts with holding ourselves and our teachers accountable by losing the idea of tenure.

I worked as an independent contractor for a seminar company, where I conducted all-day public seminars. Some people were sent and didn't want to be there, much like a student with a bad attitude. At the end of each seminar, I was evaluated by every person who attended.

It was a tough time at first, but I'm so thankful for the feedback I got. Over time, I put in the effort and improved. When I left the seminar company, I was voted fourth out of 380 trainers in the nation and first on my topic of time management.

I share this to illustrate the importance of being responsible and accountable. If I had not held myself accountable and learned to get better, I would have been asked to leave. When you make people walk the line and hold them accountable, the results are so much better.

Who benefitted from me being held accountable? I did, because I got better. And this meant my audience did too, because they enjoyed a better-quality presentation. None of us should be willing to settle for less.

Experience versus Results

What do you value more, experience or results? As I define it, *experience* is a feature and *results* are the benefit. In any business, clients are concerned with benefits and want to see results.

Experience is a nice feature, but if someone has 10 years experience and someone else 20 years, that alone doesn't indicate quality work.

For example, I was bidding on a major consulting contract, and the subject was time management. I knew I was right for this project, having once finished first in the country out of 80 people who taught that subject for my employer, the seminar company. The contract ultimately came down to just one other person and me. I lost the contract to my competitor. My greatest frustration was that I lost it because the client said the other person had more industry "experience."

I educated the client about the difference between experience and results, because you pay someone for what he or she can do for you—the result that person can achieve, not how many years of experience he or she has.

In a recent conversation with the client after the training, I asked him how it went. He said, "Okay," and then went on to tell me that he probably wouldn't use that vendor again. I later found out he is also no longer with the company. I was upset, because I knew I could have delivered the results that he wanted.

What do we practice in our organizations? Do we hold ourselves accountable? Do we preach experience to our clients, or do we preach results?

Organizations such as the NFL, NHL, or MLB recognize results more than experience. That's one of the reasons people are fans and watch the games and why the competition and talent get better every year—they are results-focused.

In organizations like our schools, some government agencies, and other groups, experience often seems to weigh heavier than results, which may account for some of the situations we find ourselves in today. Does your organization value experience more than results?

"She must be a good employee; she has 20 years of experience." Maybe she is a great employer, or maybe she has just "survived" this long.

It's on Me

My high school football coach, Dominick Ciao, had a saying that if we won a game it was our victory, but if we lost a game it was always on him. This really taught me about responsibility, in that he always took the blame and the burden when we lost a game, but he always gave us the credit and the victory when we won.

Dollars Accountable

In talking to many different businesses, I naturally come into contact with small-business owners, and I'm always amazed that many of them are working under erroneous impressions such as, "If I throw money at this problem, then it will go away," "If I hire this person, then this will happen," or "If I buy this software, my sales will increase tenfold."

The reality is that you cannot throw money at a problem and expect to be successful. Rather, you must hold your dollars accountable. Our government throws money at a problem but seldom holds our money accountable. Thus, it (and we) don't get the results it (or we) would like to get.

All business depends upon men fulfilling their responsibilities.

—Mahatma Gandhi

Source: iStockphoto. Used with permission.

Land of the Critics

We live in the land of talking heads. After every major sporting event, public speech, or just about anything, we realize that we live in a land of critics, where people are always judging others, knocking somebody down, and playing Monday morning quarterback. "This is what they should have done and this is what they need to do next time." Some of this is valuable to the audience and warranted. But it is when we constantly critique others first without looking internally that I take issue with.

We can critique someone else all day long, but at the same time many of us are not even willing to get in the game.

For example, a guy watching a football game on TV might be 50 pounds overweight, but when he sees a football player miss a tackle, he rants at that player: "Oh, my gosh! I can't believe how that guy missed him. That was ridiculous. That was one of the easiest tackles. I could have made that play. He should have had that."

This guy might never have played football and may have no idea what the physical and mental demands are. He would serve himself better if he focused on getting back into the game of health and fitness. Generally, we're easier on ourselves and harder on others. Maybe because we let our Ego get in the way. When this happened we over-estimate our ability and underestimate others.

We live in a land of critiques, so before we judge others, let's do an internal look first.

> *It is not the critic who counts: not the man who points out how the strong man stumbles or where the doer of deeds could have done better. The credit belongs to the man who is actually in the arena, whose face is marred by dust and sweat and blood, who strives valiantly, who errs and comes up short again and again, because there is no effort without error or shortcoming, but who knows the great enthusiasms, the great devotions, who spends himself for a worthy cause; who, at the best, knows, in the end, the triumph of high achievement, and who, at the worst, if he fails, at least he fails while daring greatly, so that his place shall never be with those cold and timid souls who knew neither victory nor defeat.*
>
> —Theodore Roosevelt

Teaching Accountability

A segment of our population, Generation Y, is called the entitlement generation, because they have not been held accountable for most of their life. Helicopter parents have hovered over them, and it is just assumed that Mom or Dad rescued them whenever they got into trouble. The "they can do no wrong" attitude has crippled them, and it is crippling our society.

When you don't teach someone to be responsible or if someone doesn't learn how to be accountable at an early age, that person has a very different learning curve. Here are four ways to teach accountability to a young person.

1. **Demonstrate accountability.** If you are a parent, teacher, coach, or mentor, you have a responsibility to demonstrate accountability. For example, if you say, "The meeting starts at 5 PM," make sure that you arrive 5 minutes earlier. Model the behavior that you want from others.

2. **Put it in writing.** Put the expectation you have for a student or the person you are working with in writing and let him or her sign it, because the level of commitment goes up when someone puts his or her name to it in writing.

3. **Remind periodically.** "I'm going to hold you accountable, because this needs to be turned in on (such and such date)." Periodically, people need reminders, whether it's a written or verbal reminder or one posted in a classroom.

4. **Set up consequences and hold the person accountable.** We lose accountability in our society when we waver. "If you make this grade, then you can go on this trip, and if not, then you can't go."

For example, a dad has this conversation with his daughter: "Sara, you didn't get a good grade on your math test. You got a D, so you can't sleep over at Becky's house tonight." But Dad has been away all week and feels guilty for not being with Sara, so he ultimately lets her go to Becky's and doesn't hold her accountable for her bad grade.

What does Sara learn from this experience? Unfortunately, she probably learns that she won't be held accountable for her future actions, because there are no consequences.

Leadership Tip

Holding ourselves and others accountable will lead us on a path to accomplishing our goals.

5 | Building a High-Trust Team

The Power of Teamwork

In 1979, a man gathered a group of young men in a room and said to them: "You're going to make history. What you're going to do is shock the world."

These young men thought to themselves, "What is this guy talking about, making history, shocking the world?" But on February 22, 1980, in Lake Placid, New York, that's exactly what they did when an announcer asked, "Do you believe in miracles?"

That man was coach Herb Brooks of the 1980 Men's Olympic Gold hockey team, where the average age of the players was 21 years. It was composed of amature hockey players who took on the Soviet team, who was one of the best teams in the world at the time.

They did it with the power of teamwork; when you combine 1 + 1 and it doesn't add up to 2 but to sums greater than that, when you don't work as individuals but as a team, as a unit you can do great things.

We see the importance of teamwork in many companies today, such as 3M, Federal Express, GE, Toyota, and Johnson & Johnson.

Individual commitment to a group effort—that is what makes a team work, a company work, a society work, a civilization work.
                                                                    —Vince Lombardi

The Importance of Teamwork

There are two reasons why teamwork is a must in business and in society today: increased competition and limited resources. We are no longer competing only among ourselves in the United States. We are competing with many nations, including Japan, China, and India—all of which are now making their way onto the world stage for our jobs and our dollars.

In recent decades we have seen US jobs go overseas. Just pick up a newspaper or turn on a TV to understand that our economy is now part of a global marketplace.

Frequently I hear, "Eric, I'm getting asked to do more with less," but I haven't met anyone who is getting more money or resources and actually doing less. On the contrary, we see people who are being asked to do more and to do more with less. As a result, teamwork becomes critical to succeed in business and maintain a competitive advantage.

Why Teams Fail in the Workplace

Teams fail in the workplace for three reasons:

1. **There is no team-building concept.** Instead, we find a group of five to seven individuals who have been thrust together and told, "You all work together; we want you to achieve (the stated goal)." The group rarely forms because they never got to know one another and experienced a bond or established trust, and as such, it becomes very difficult to achieve a common goal. There is no emphasis or training for teamwork and team building.
2. **The goals are unclear.** Unclear goals are usually a result of people bringing their own agendas and goals into the team goal, thus diluting the team and making the primary goal very difficult to achieve.
3. **There is a lack of management support.** Without support, they aren't given the authority to make decisions necessary for the team's success.

Trust Defined

I define *trust* as "belief," but many people define it differently. The word *trust* is used in the media, in magazines, and on TV.

You hear the word *trust* used often, but sometimes it is used incorrectly.

Trust is not predicting someone's outcome. For example, "I trust Bob is going to do this in the meeting today." (Trust is not predicting someone's actions.) This is how trust can be misused.

Defined as belief, trust means that I believe in you. And if I believe in you, my belief comes in two parts. One is that I believe in your ability, if we're working together on a team, and the second part is that I believe you have my interest and the team's best interest at hand.

Trust is important because it exists everywhere in our society, including, for example, in banking. The next time you go online to check your statement, consider the amount of trust you put into your bank. It's a great amount of trust, especially if you put all of your funds in one bank. So your level of trust with that bank should be fairly high.

We trust our health care professionals, our dentists, and our doctors when we put our health concerns in their hands. Essentially we say to them, "We trust in your ability and that you have our best interests at stake."

We see trust, and sometimes a lack of it, in government, business, and education, as well as in families. Trust plays an important role in family dynamics, especially when trust is broken.

Leadership Tip: Trust in the Workplace

I define *trust* and how to establish it in the workplace with the acronym **TRUST**:

T: Talk straight
R: Relationships
U: Understanding
S: Show face
T: Time

Talk Straight

Talking straight simply means saying what you mean and meaning what you say. Here's an example of why straight talk is important: I wanted to buy a condo, and a property manager was showing me a particular property, describing its intricacies and telling me how nice it was. "Yes, we have a lot of young professionals moving in here. It's a very nice place. We have a pool. It's got a fitness center."

Then I asked her a very simple question, "Do you live here?"

She didn't answer my question the first time, so I asked a second time, thinking she might not have heard me correctly. "Do you live here?"

She totally avoided it, so I asked her a third time. By then I was becoming annoyed and again asked, "Do you live here?"

She said, "Well, to be honest with you, I live here from time to time."

Say What You Mean
and
Mean What You Say

Then I said to her, "'To be honest with me'? So you weren't honest with me before this?"

And she replied, "Oh, that's just the way I talk."

After she said that, I felt so uneasy that I got in my car and left; I never bought the condo. If she didn't live at that property, she simply could have told me either, "I don't live here," or, "I live here three days out of the month." I would have been okay with any honest, straightforward answer.

As she dodged the answer, I felt increasingly uneasy and started to lose trust in her and what she said. If she gave me a half-answer on this question, what else would she give me a half-answer on as well?

When you say you will do something, make sure you do it. Your word is your truth—in business and in life. If you say you'll be somewhere at a certain time, make sure you're there. Straight talk and keeping your word says you are someone others can trust, and your reputation depends on it.

Relationships

Trust is like a relationship. It takes devotion of time and attention. Relationships exist in many forms, and everyone has his or her own history with trust issues. Some may have been burned in the past, as people let them down, and might not trust so easily, whereas others more readily give their trust. For example, it might take two months to establish trust with Bob in accounting but two years with Joe in HR.

Understanding

Trust involves understanding that everyone is different and will have unique opinions and viewpoints on any given topic. Respecting a person's views, personality style, and personal history gives you greater insight to establish trust with him or her. But it can't be forced, and your interest in the other person must always be sincere and based on trust.

Show Face

The world-famous Mardi Gras parade takes place each year in
New Orleans, Louisiana. Some people expose themselves in the
hope of getting beads. Now, I'm not saying to expose yourself to
your colleagues at work, but I am suggesting that you open up to
people and allow them into parts of your world.

How do you open up? One way is to admit your mistakes.
Tell somebody, "Hey, I'm not that good at this. You're better at
this than I am."

Another great way of opening up is to ask for help. Les Brown
is a motivational speaker and National Speakers Association (NSA)
colleague. One of his quotes that I love deals with having the
courage to ask for help: "Ask for help, not because you're weak,
but because you want to remain strong."

Having the courage to open up or admit mistakes shows that
you're human and paves a way for others to trust you. "This person
is not trying to pull the wool over my eyes. They're showing face.
They're opening up. That's a courageous act."

Time

Developing trust takes time and requires that you put in the time
to establish trust with someone.

I once got a phone call from a vice president of sales about
doing a training session for his group. He told me how his people
didn't trust one another and they didn't trust him, so I asked him
a very simple question, "Do you trust them?"

He responded, "No, but they need to get along and start
trusting each other." He kept putting the blame on them.

I replied: "I can come and entertain them, and they can leave
feeling inspired and motivated, but the result will be the same unless
you open up to them. Unless you start spending time with them,
asking for help, getting to know them and start talking straight to
them, trust will not be established and problems will continue."

Building Trust

Some people at work seem to annoy us to no end, and we just don't get along, but generally they don't annoy us out of spite. Often, personality styles differ and conflict in certain areas, which can disrupt productivity and adversely affect careers. Personality Assessments can help build trust. To know and understand the personality styles of coworkers can promote a greater sense of trust, especially among team members.

A good way to build trust in these groups is to take a personality inventory, administered by an authorized company or other qualified professional. This way, everyone can have an understanding of his or her team members' personalities without having to diagnose them.

Two personality test options are the Myers-Briggs Type Indicator and the DiSC Personality Profile.

Another way to build trust is get to know other people, including their likes and their hobbies. Patrick Lencioni is a colleague who wrote *Overcoming the Five Dysfunctions of a Team: A Field Guide,* in which he gives great examples to build trust, as well as related activity suggestions.

My definition of a team is a group of individuals working as one to achieve a common objective. Just as I use an acronym for TRUST, I also use one for building a high-trust team: **TEAM:**

T: Trust
E: Environment
A: Accountability
M: Measured results

Trust

We've discussed the merits of trust and how it relates to a team, so we'll skip ahead to consider the other elements of TEAM.

Environment

The environment can be separated into two distinct parts: an environment capable of having healthy conflict and a motivating environment. Let's first discuss components of healthy conflict.

Healthy conflict is being able to debate with someone on an issue. Where healthy conflict exists, healthy decision making is also present. Conversely, a boring meeting equals bad results. Engaging in healthy debate fosters interaction in meetings and team environments.

Conversely, have you ever been in a team setting where the boss says, "This quarter we're going to achieve (Objective A) and go after (Target B). Any questions?" and then nobody said anything? Instead, everyone just sat there saying, "Yes, that's good."

Then, as soon as you leave the meeting, a colleague approaches you in the hallway and says, "That's never going to happen. I don't know what he's talking about, but he's way off base."

This example represents unhealthy conflict, defined as getting emotionally involved, engaging in name-calling, or calling someone out and becoming more focused on the other person than on the issue.

The environment should motivate people, but before continuing, consider three questions you should ask every member of your team:

1. *What are your values?* (What qualities do they value? Do they value family?)
2. *What are your likes, your hobbies?*
3. *What motivates you?* (Ask and you'll find a variety of answers such as, "I'm motivated by having flex time," "I'm motivated when nobody bothers me," or "I'm motivated when someone just comes up to me and gives me recognition.")

There are two things that people want more than sex and money . . . recognition and praise.

—Mary Kay Ash

Now let's discuss how to create a motivating environment based on the following seven points:

1. **Recognize people (five coins technique).** A great way to create an environment that motivates is to use the five coins technique. This technique allows you to create an environment that recognizes people for their good efforts or deeds.

   When dressing for the day, put five coins in your right pocket or on your desk. Then throughout the day, find people you believe deserve a compliment and tell them. Make sure that the compliment is specific and sincere. Then transfer a coin from your right pocket into your left pocket. At the end of the day the goal is to give five compliments and have no more coins in your right pocket.

   Failure to recognize people has negative consequences. My brother told me the story about someone at his company. A man he knew and looked up to had finally had enough. He was leaving his job, and one of the reasons was a lack of recognition from his boss. During his more than five years at the company, the boss never said "good job" on any project or activity, which is sad because the employee probably would have stayed if he felt appreciated.

   Although people go to work for a paycheck, they also want to be appreciated. When you create an environment where people are appreciated and collect a paycheck, you create a motivating environment. The five coins technique will help you get there.

2. **Use thank-you notes.** These days, you probably receive thank-you notes via e-mail. And how many e-mails do you get a day? Many, I'm sure. Sending handwritten thank-you notes on a consistent basis motivates team members to perform better and boosts deeper levels of communication. Do you still have some type of thank-you note that is several years old?

We can do no great things; only small things with great love.
—Mother Teresa

3. **Have fun.** Creating an environment where people actually have fun may require some ingenuity in your role as team boss, but levity and fun also have their place in business. Relaxing a bit lifts most everyone's attitude about work and getting along with teammates. Focusing on goals is certainly important, but creating an atmosphere that's fun produces good results when managed properly.

4. **Create an award.** Creating an awards system strengthens your business, because it shows appreciation for your employees. And you can create one whether you're in customer service or sales. Jim Ziegler, a friend and popular legend in the auto industry, gives dealership sales managers a four-foot-tall trophy; they then award it to a top salesperson each month.

   Have something unique, like a golden telephone. A lady in one of my seminars was in charge of a call center and got her husband to repaint old telephones the color of gold. Each month she gives out a gold telephone award, which sets her business apart from others.

5. **Buy someone's lunch.** Food brings people together and gets them talking. A favorite interactive way to motivate the work environment is to take people to lunch or sponsor a team lunch. Holding a company picnic where everyone brings a favorite dish, combined with team activities, encourages teams to work together more effectively.

6. **Give away $5 gift cards.** This encourages employees by rewarding them with a token of recognition. It also inspires greater competition. Careful budgeting keeps fiscal goals intact.

7. **Show people how they make a difference to your business.** This is one of the best ways to create a motivating environment. I see many teams working very hard to accomplish their goals, going from one goal to the next. Take time to celebrate success and acknowledge everyone's efforts.

Stopping to celebrate what you have accomplished together also allows time to evaluate what is and isn't working. "This person worked well with that person. This person didn't work so well over here, so let's change that."

Two great books on how to create a motivating environment are *1001 Ways to Motivate and Reward Your Employees,* by Bob Nelson, and *The Carrot Principle,* by Adrian Gostick and Chester Elton.

Accountability

Accountability is essential to building a high-trust team. It forces you to grow and moves you from achieving okay results to achieving amazing results. Do you hold yourself and team members accountable?

A great way to hold yourself accountable is to have a written daily results list that includes, for example, what you did today and what you accomplished. Having an accountability partner holds you responsible for sticking to a daily results list that others can see and evaluate.

As a personal trainer, I often trained couples who lived together. As accountability partners, they showed up and worked out together to achieve their fitness goals and keep each other on the right track, as opposed to neither showing up if one person didn't feel like working out.

Holding yourself and team members accountable is very important for a team's success. One of the biggest questions I get, whether from midlevel managers or regional vice presidents, is, "Eric, how do I get my folks to hold themselves accountable?"

You must hold yourself accountable and also have someone in your organization to hold you accountable. Starting at the top sets a good example for teams being accountable to you and one another.

One of the biggest reasons we went through the 2009 financial crisis is because leaders stopped holding themselves accountable.

Accountability exists in sports. We call it the scoreboard or record. We need the same in organizations.

Some organizations have accountability for departments, in terms of revenue they generate. If your company doesn't have an accountability system, ask about developing one, because holding people accountable increases performance and results.

Measured Results

Having measured results is having clear goals and expectations, what some people call the scoreboard. This can be an important part of a team's success. Make sure you have your team's scoreboard in two key areas. The first area is the financial scoreboard: Did we achieve this goal financially? The second area includes: Did we achieve the goal? How did we work well together? Are we getting along? and Are we making progress?

Why We Join Teams

> Men Wanted: For hazardous journey. Small wages, bitter cold, long months of complete darkness, constant danger, safe return doubtful. Honor and recognition in case of success.
>
> —Sir Ernest Shackleton

Sir Ernest Shackleton posted this notice as he gathered a crew for the voyage to the Antarctic continent. The next day, hundreds of young men lined up hoping to be selected. I recommend reading this incredible story of teamwork, of how all the men survived bitter cold and returned home. It symbolizes human's desire to be part of something bigger than the self.

Team Building—Life or Death

On August 5, 2010, news spread around the world that 33 miners were trapped 2,300 feet below earth. On October 13, 2010, 69 days later, the same 33 trapped men rose from the mine. All had lived.

One of the miners was quoted as saying, "I'm just one link in the chain," thus emphasizing the importance of team building and teamwork in such a situation.

As a Chilean psychiatrist was interviewed, she cited team building as a key attribute that kept the men alive; it allowed them to create an organized structure, enabled them to work together, and helped them share their scant amount of food. Team building played a vital role in helping to save their lives.

> *Teamwork is the ability to work together toward a common vision; the ability to direct individual accomplishments toward organizational objectives. It is the fuel that allows common people to attain uncommon results.*
>
> —Andrew Carnegie

6

Leading in
Any Position

You . . . a Person of Influence, a Leader

Have you ever asked yourself who has influenced you? Perhaps it was a neighbor, a teacher, a coach, a coworker, a colleague, a friend, a relative, a spouse or partner, a parent, or a child. Have you ever asked whom do you influence? Chances are you have influenced someone in those same groups mentioned.

A major element of leadership is to realize that you are a person of influence. Leadership is not about a title or a position. It's about a choice you make to be a person of influence, to carry yourself in a certain regard so that others will follow you.

Consider the kind of life you lead, the kinds of decisions you make, and with whom you hang around and associate. In doing so, you begin to realize that you are a person who influences others.

Two words come to mind when I consider the term *leadership:* *followers* and *influence*. Leadership means that you have followers, and if you have followers, then you have some form of influence. The most powerful people are those with the most influence.

A leader is someone who has followers and is influential over them. Leadership inspires others to say things like: "I'd follow him anywhere," "She lives her message," and "He's not afraid to do the hard work and lead by example."

In my seminars I use the following example: I take a $1 bill out of one pocket and say, "Somebody comes to you and this $1 bill represents her current skill set."

Pulling out a $100 bill from my other pocket I'd say, "Your job as a leader is to take that $1 and turn it into $100, where it's profitable not only for your organization but also for the other person by helping her further develop her talents and skill set. Then she is able to help someone else in that same regard."

Values and Voice

Leadership is also about finding your internal voice in terms of values. What do you stand for? What relationships do you value? Family? Friends? What is your internal guide system for making decisions? What is your moral compass?

Before you begin working for an organization, examine your values. That way, if something comes up in your personal life or at work that conflict with your values, you can make a decision and stand by it. If not, circumstances can become very tricky.

For example, the owner of a printing company told me a story about a gentleman I'll call Mike. Mike accepted the position of general manager at that company. Mike was a Christian and deeply rooted in his beliefs. Jobs came in to print girls in skimpy bathing suits and scantily clad clothes, and he was having a real disconnect with this.

Instead of talking to the company owner and saying, "This is really not the position for me; it goes against my beliefs," he decided to call the customer and try to persuade him to not print the images and to go another route. Not only did it upset the customer, but it also upset the company owner, and Mike was asked to leave the position. I commend Mike for taking a stand for what he believes, but he should have had that discussion with the owner and not the customer.

Before you find yourself in a similar position, determine your values before potentially being involved in a compromising situation.

Qualities of Highly Regarded Leaders

The book *The Leadership Challenge,* fourth edition, by James M. Kouzes and Barry Z. Posner, presents an interesting study of 75,000 people worldwide covering six continents. When interviewed, people were asked, "What should a leader be, and what qualities do you want a leader to have?"

Following, in the order of importance, are the four most cited leadership qualities:

1. **Honest:** A leader should be honest and trustworthy, someone who does whatever he or she says and who speaks the truth rather than trying to pull the wool over others' eyes.
2. **Forward-looking:** This means having the ability to look ahead, to have a vision for where the leaders of an organization are taking their people.
3. **Inspiring:** Inspiration happens when you communicate vision to others. It can be found in a speech you're giving or by the life you live.
4. **Competent:** A leader must be competent, someone with the right skill set or someone who has a track record of getting results and achieving success.

Leaders Care

Make Recognition
Specific and Sincere

It's important to be smart, effective, results-based, and results-focused, but it's more important to connect with someone on an emotional level, with someone you care about and hold a deep appreciation for and whom you regard as a person rather than a number or just to fill in a spot.

I've created the acronym for CARE. It stands for these four ideas:

C: Climate
A: Accountability
R: Recognition
E: Empowerment

People don't care how much you know until they know how much you care.

—Anonymous

To be a truly effective leader you must demonstrate that you care for those that you lead.

Climate

Be sure that the climate in your organization is a high-trust and high-communication environment, where people feel safe to connect and share information and ideas.

Accountability

Great leaders take full responsibility for defeat and share victories. A personal story describes accountability:

While driving back from Ft. Lauderdale, I stopped to get gas around Exit 173, just short of my destination at Exit 199. But when I got back on the interstate I was preoccupied. The next thing I knew, I was looking at the sign for Exit 243. "How did I miss this exit?" I thought. "I don't even remember seeing a sign for 199. It must not have been big enough."

Then it hit me: I can either say it's Florida's fault—they should have had a bigger sign—or I can look inwardly and say it's my fault—and that I missed it because I was on the phone with a friend.

I acknowledged that it was my fault, and I ended up laughing about it later with a friend.

People always blame their "circumstances" for what they are. I don't believe in such circumstances. The people who get on in this world are those who get up and look for the circumstances they want . . . and if they can't find them, then they make them happen.

—George Bernard Shaw

Recognition

Great leaders recognize their employees. Two common reasons employees leave a job are because their bosses don't recognize them or because they micromanage or "snoopervise" their employees. Employees want respect and recognition for what they contribute, not just their paycheck.

I once gave a seminar in Orlando, Florida, and asked the audience, "How long do you think recognition lasts?"

A lady's hand shot up and she said, "My boss recognized me two months ago and has never said anything before that she liked the quality of my work; it still feels good to this day to even think about it."

I said, "Wow, that's excellent. Thanks for sharing that." I also said, "Shame on your boss for waiting so long to recognize you." Don't hoard recognition, but when you give it, make sure that it is specific and sincere.

Celebration accompanies recognition, so take time to celebrate victories when they occur. When I taught project management, I was often surprised that many managers never actually celebrated a completed project or a major assignment. They simply moved on to the next task. Always celebrate your accomplishments.

Empowerment

Great leaders delegate power that is focused on the results and not the process. A great example of this comes from Captain D. Michael Abrashoff and his command of USS *Benfold*. He is the author of *It's Your Ship,* which is a great book about what happens when you empower people. He was able to lead effectively because he empowered everyone on the ship.

Imposed versus Respected Influence

Do people respect you because of the title you hold or for who you are regardless of title?

Imposed influence is having to follow someone simply because of the title that follows that person's name. You might not respect the person, but you have to take orders from him or her because that person is your boss.

Respected influence is having people follow you who generally respect you. They feel as if they don't want to let you down. They respect you for who you are and the title you hold.

Better results are more likely to happen in a situation where a team follows a leader out of mutual respect. Respected influence fosters team cohesiveness, allowing the team to grow, share ideas, and achieve success—and titles remain secondary.

The Importance of a Name

Everyone's name is important. Do you know the name of the person who cleans your building? People like to hear the sound of their own name. As a leader, it's important to realize this and make a concerted effort to learn an employee's name, as well as the names of those important in their lives, such as a spouse or a child. Learning names shows that you actually care about others as people.

When I speak before an audience of fewer than 80 people and have time before my speech, I make an effort to learn everyone's name. It's my way of showing appreciation for them for being there. It also shows that I want to get to know them personally, and frequently, I may use their story or some of their comments in my talk.

Listening and Asking Questions

An effective leader may not be the smartest person or know all the answers, but that person does know how to listen and ask questions of employees and then listen to their input.

Did you ever drive to a gas station and ask for directions before the age of GPS devices and cell phones to tell you where to go? Did you get directions and then find yourself back in the car and lost again? If you've ever wondered about this, it's related to our ability to ask good questions.

Effective communication starts with good listening skills and the ability to ask good questions. Most of us do a terrible job of asking questions. Either we don't ask questions, or we don't ask the right questions. Instead of asking someone for landmarks, like a gas station, we quickly get back in our car only to find ourselves lost again.

The benefits of asking good questions save you time and more work, give you a better understanding, increase your chances of success, and put you in control of the conversation. Asking better questions of those you lead is part of being an effective communicator.

The Company You Keep

My mom is pretty sharp. She has a master's degree in teaching and taught school all her life. She always told my brothers and me that who you hang around with is who you become; birds of a feather flock together. And that's so true of a leader and anyone who sees himself or herself as a leader.

Leaders surround themselves with positive, uplifting people who are winners. Enthusiasm is contagious, but so are whining and negativity. Leaders need to be friendly with everyone, but they can't be everyone's friend. Realize that not everyone will agree with some of your decisions.

Do you surround yourself with those who have a different viewpoint than you? Abraham Lincoln, the sixteenth president of the United States, was known for associating with people who didn't share his viewpoint; he did so because it helped him see the other side of issues.

Consider those you associate with and realize that often these are the people you become.

Keep Your Word

I once saw a TV interview with Jon Huntsman, founder of Huntsman Corporation, a publicly traded billion-dollar company. He was being interviewed on the *Glenn Beck Show,* where he told a story about keeping his word.

In 1985, Jon Huntsman sold 40 percent of the shares in his company to Great Lakes Chemical for $54 million. He and Great Lakes Chemical chief executive officer (CEO), Emerson Kampen, shook hands on the deal.

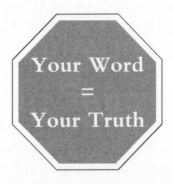

Lawyers for both companies worked on the details, and it took about six months before all the legal documents were prepared.

During this time, profits increased in Huntsman's company and business got a lot better. It was now estimated to be worth about $250 million, yet Mr. Huntsman was selling it for $54 million.

Mr. Kampen came back and said, "Jon, I understand your company is worth a lot more than $54 million. I'm willing to give you more money for it. Just tell me what I need to do."

Jon Huntsman looked him in the eye and said, "I shook your hand for $54 million and that's all I expect you to pay me."

This was the start of a great relationship between the two men. Mr. Huntsman even spoke at Mr. Kampen's funeral.

Demanding versus Demeaning

Sometimes it's easy to demand something of someone, like a deadline or a project that's due, but be careful to not cross the line between being demanding and demeaning.

I once hosted a session for a celebrity speaker at a hotel. This person has many great qualities, but the one negative quality was that he was not afraid to use certain language when talking to hotel employees.

Although his language may not have been abusive, it certainly may have offended some people. It made me ask if that type of language was really necessary and prompted me to consider the line between being demanding and being demeaning.

Being demanding can be beneficial, because it raises the level of expectations from those around you, but demeaning someone only hurts that individual and negatively influences that person's desire to work for you next time.

It's one thing to be demanding and to have high expectations from those around you, but it's not acceptable to be demeaning.

What Energy Do You Carry?

People may or may not remember what you say or did, but they will always remember how you made them feel. Have you ever noticed when people enter a room, they bring a type of energy with them?

For example, you're at your cubicle talking with someone when another person approaches you and you get a feeling of, "Oh great, I'm so glad he's coming." Or maybe it's a feeling of, "Oh man, he's coming over here. Let me wrap up my conversation and get the heck out of here before he comes, because he's either going to say something I don't like, put me down, or try to make me feel inferior."

What energy do you carry when you enter a room? Are you a person who brightens the room up upon entering? Or are you bringing in storm clouds?

GOOO—Get Out of Office!

One of the most effective ways to be a good leader is to get out of the office. A popular phrase is "managing by wandering around." Sometimes we spend too much time in meetings or behind closed doors working on our own material we think is so important, but it may not be.

The people in your organization make your organization work, and when you get out of the office you build relationships with your employees, in part because they actually see you. And when people see you several times a week, your words have more meaning and their trust in you increases.

Another advantage is that you can listen better to what is going on with your employees and you are better able to give feedback on the spot. So get out of your office, visit with your colleagues, and continue to build those relationships.

Tell Me What I Don't Want to Hear

Often when I conduct seminars, people approach me and say, "Eric, this information is great, but I can't tell my boss or my manager that, because they only want to hear what they want to hear." And that's a shame, because as the leader of your organization, you want to hear everything, not just what is nice or pleasant. Hearing everything allows you to take a proactive approach.

Once while traveling, I was in a restaurant for lunch, and the owner working the cash register said, "If you like our restaurant tell everybody, and if you don't like it, don't tell anyone."

I thought, "That's the dumbest thing I've heard all day."

As the owner he should say, "If you don't like something, I want to be the first to know."

Most business owners want to know how to improve their businesses. When you essentially say, "Just tell me what I want to know," you limit yourself for growth, for what you can accomplish, and the results you can see.

Business owners absolutely need feedback. Comments may not be pleasant to hear every time, but feedback is necessary in order to improve, keep clients coming, and attract new customers.

Your most unhappy customers are your greatest source of learning.
—Bill Gates

Leadership Self-Talk

Does this sound familiar? "I'm an idiot, I have a terrible memory, and I can't do that." If so, stop that negative thinking, because the thoughts you tell yourself are powerful. As a leader and person of influence, you must be mindful of what you tell yourself; the mind believes what you tell it.

Your body is a massive ship of potential, influenced and directed by a little voice inside you. What does your little voice tell you, for example, when you awake in the morning? "I feel terrific," or "Do I have to get up?"

When you look in the mirror, what does that little voice say? "I look and feel great," or, "I wish I had more hair."

What does it say when you interact with people? "How can I help this person?" or "I already know what he's going to say."

Self-talk is important and beneficial, and it's very important to monitor your self-talk. If not, you potentially fall victim to negative self-talk. So give internal self-talk with positive affirmations such as:

- "Today is going to be an awesome day."
- "I feel terrific."
- "I'll stick to my plan."
- "I have an amazing memory."
- "I bring passion and enthusiasm to my work."
- "I expect good things to happen."

You become what you constantly tell yourself, and as a leader, you must build yourself up, especially when trying to build up others.

7

Leading the Entitlement Generation

Who Is Generation Y?

A generation is a group of individuals born in the same time period who exhibit similar behaviors and share similar life experiences. Generation Y is a group of individuals born between the mid to late 1970s and the early 2000s. There are more than 70 million people in this generation, one of the largest generations in history. Other names for Generation Y include Millennials, Generation Next, the Nintendo Generation, Echo Boomers, and the Me Generation.

Characteristics of Generation Y include:

- Tech savvy
- Multitask-oriented
- Educated (one of the most educated generations in history)
- Team player
- Diverse
- Optimistic
- Entrepreneurial
- Goal-focused
- Lifestyle-driven
- Big spender
- Environment-friendly
- Talented
- Influential

The last time you bought a computer, whom did you consult? Was it a young person in your family? If not, you might have gone to your local Best Buy and bought that computer from a person in the Generation Y age bracket. This generation likes technology. Some of their thoughts about work are:

- "I want to see my ideas implemented."
- "I like to work for people who respect me and listen to me."
- "My boss told me that it will take two years before my first advancement, but little does he know that I'll be on Monster this afternoon."
- "I like to work with others on a project."

- "Nobody around here seems to know what I can do to get ahead."

Some events that define Generation Y include the White House scandal, the O.J. Simpson car chase and trial, the Columbine shooting, the home run race and steroids in baseball, the Iraq and Gulf wars, corporate scandals like Enron, Arthur Andersen and WorldCom, and outsourcing jobs.

Three Other Generations

Three other generations that make up our consumer and workplace demographic are the Veteran Generation, the Baby Boomers, and Generation X.

- **Veterans were born between 1930 and 1945.** This generation grew up listening to programs on the radio; they were defined by FDR, his presidency, and the New Deal; the fear of war and of Germany; and the Great Depression. The Veteran Generation is concerned with engaging in face-to-face interactions, listening, and being patient. Generally, they keep active and want others to know that they are still young at heart and valuable in society.
- **Baby Boomers were born between 1946 and 1964**. They are known as a workaholic generation, and society can thank many of them for the 60-hour workweek. They are defined by the civil rights movement, the Vietnam War, the Beatles, and landing on the moon. Baby Boomers are a very optimistic generation that cares about income earning power, status and title, and, now, being able to telecommunicate.
- **The Generation X population was born between 1965 and 1977.** They are a skeptical generation known as latch key kids and generally are very independent.

Events that define them were the Nixon Watergate scandal, the AIDS epidemic, the tearing down of the Berlin Wall, MTV, the tragic launch pad explosion of NASA's Apollo 1 module killing three American astronauts, and the home computer. Balance, total compensation and benefits, and company culture are important to them.

Generation Y and Entitlement

Why is Generation Y defined as having a sense of entitlement? A young woman told me a story that sums it up pretty well. After my presentation at a realtors' association, she quickly came up and told me that when her niece comes for a visit, they always go to Bonefish Grill (a mid- to high-price restaurant). When I asked, "Is it because it's your niece's birthday you're eating out or any special occasion."

The lady said, "No, she's just so accustomed to going there, that every time she comes over we just take her there."

I asked, "Does she order off the kid's menu, because she's just a kid?"

And she replied, "No, she's seven years old, and she orders right off the adult menu."

This is how the entitlement can start at an early age. It's because we open the door for these types of situations and give them unilateral decision-making power. They then take that power into other situations and eventually go to work, expecting to make similar types of unilateral decisions.

Latitude for special occasions like birthdays is understandable, but allowing youngsters such latitude inflates their sense of power. This sense of entitlement often makes it very difficult for teachers and managers to lead this generation.

Recruiting and Retaining Generation Y

The first way that a business can recruit Generation Y workers is to be a great company with a great brand. The best way to retain them is to be an employer of choice. People from Generation Y choose their employers like the brand of clothes they wear. They want to be proud of the company so that they can tell their friends and associate with those of influence.

Another great way to recruit and retain Generation Yers is to take a look at your current management staff. How good are your managers? If you want to retain the best Generation Y talent, you must have managers who can scout talent as well as develop people.

In scouting talent, determine that your management staff is a good judge of talent. This step should never be overlooked. An excellent guide to follow is to examine how consistently well-performing sports teams scout for good talent.

I'd rather have a lot of good talent and a little experience than a lot of experience and a little talent.

—John Wooden

Ultimately, the manager will be working with your new hire. You have to help that manager identify key types of talent pertinent to your job and industry.

These days, human resources (HR) plays too much of a role in hiring new people. Managers should have the majority vote, because they will be responsible for developing and working with new hires.

It is in developing talent that your manager will be transformed from manager to coach/teacher. Generation Yers grew up with coaches and teachers in sports and other activities, and just because someone has a title or specific role doesn't mean anything. This population wants actual results.

Ask yourself, "Can my managers coach people? Do they coach well? Are they good at identifying someone's strengths? And if not, what are the skills I need to work on with my managers?"

Generation Y workers want to acquire new skills and be on the cutting edge, so you need managers who can scout the talent and also develop it. In looking at recruiting and retaining Generation Yers, you might be losing candidates due to poor management, because Generation Y workers will not put up with this situation.

Someone once told me, "Eric, I had a great employee, 23 years old, but he left my company to go and do this." So what?

Generation Yers are just trying to feel their way through life, to identify themselves and who they are. They might go to another company, but they will always want to keep the door open, which means they might even come back.

A great company will always attract good people. It's a simple rule. But you must be willing to change your mind-set and keep the Generation Y relationship open—because if a great Generation Yer leaves, you can ask that person to refer someone else.

Another great way to recruit and retain Generation Y is to look at current positions in your organization and see how you can make them independent contractors. Generation Y is a big fan of their free time and their social life, and it's not necessary to nail them down for a 9 to 5 or 8 to 4 workday every day. Sometimes companies place too much emphasis on how many hours someone worked as opposed to the results one has produced.

If possible, see how you can create independent contractor (IC) positions so that they can work from home, or work 20+ hours per week, and then pay them on that level. ICs are paid for their results, not for their time sitting in a chair. Look for creative ways people can work from home while still being an employee of your company.

Earning salary is very important to a young or older person. A great way to recruit and retain Generation Yers is to pay for actual results rather than be too concerned with their experience or the process. "I expect this, and if you can get it for me, I will pay you this." By paying well, you have a better chance of attracting and keeping a valuable employee.

Choosing the Right Generation Y Worker

There are two types of Generation Y workers, and you need to identify which type of worker (employee) you want to attract.

I once worked with a Generation Y friend who sold commercial real estate. He was really gung-ho and wanted to be the best and stand out in his company. For several Saturdays we worked on his sales presentation, his market strategies, and his target market. He was very driven.

Another friend of mine would be the second type of worker. He works at our local fitness club. After his first two weeks of working there, everything was going okay. A month later I asked him how things were going at the fitness club.

His response: "Oh, not so good. They didn't allow me to take off when I had to go to a wedding, so I just ended up walking out."

Those are perfect examples of the two types of Generation Y prospects. One type is willing to give it their all and can't see their name outside in lights fast enough. In the other group, work is more of a hobby, and they haven't found anything about the job that excites them. So choose wisely.

Managing Generation Y

Generation Y folks are goal-oriented and move quickly. Taught by their parents and teachers to set goals and aim high, they grew up with information available to them in a matter of minutes. As a manager of Generation Y employees, you must show them what they are working toward and why their position is important.

One way is to have value-driven goals. This shows Generation Y the integrity of your company and your commitment to something greater than just making money. This goal impresses them in a big way, as they are one of the most volunteer-oriented generations in history and have an honest concern for the environment.

The second goal is to have a measurable set of tangible goals, where they can actually see progress being made and the results. Provide a motivating environment with clearly outlined goals that both you, as manager, and the employee agree to, mapping out mutual goals on a weekly or monthly basis.

Generation Y workers like a structured environment with clear expectations and identified goals. This is not the same as a bureaucratic environment. Generation Yers like enough structure for both discipline and creativity to come together. They want to work for a company that is organized and provides structure. They thrive in this type of environment, because it resembles the familiar, secure environment of their youth and adolescence.

Generation Yers are generally excited to go to work. Contrary to what others may think, they want to work for a company where not only are their ideas heard but they can contribute. They have contributed ideas their whole life, from their parents asking them where they wanted to go to eat to their parents asking what type of computer they should buy.

Generation Y Hierarchy of Needs

Personal
Growth

Belief in Company

Actual Contribution

Fun Environment

Feel Needed

- **Level 1: Necessities Met.** Generation Yers want to be in an environment where *their necessities can be met.* It's important for them to have a paycheck to pay for their cell phone, car payment, apartment rent, or weekend spending habits.
- **Level 2: Fun Work Environment.** Generation Yers want to be in a situation where they enjoy going to work and where they have friends.
- **Level 3: Actual Contribution to the Organization.** Do Generation Yers know that what they are doing is important? Do they see their role as crucial to the company's success? They want to see that they are not just a number, but rather a vital part of the organization.
- **Level 4: Belief in the Company**. At this stage, Generation Y workers will brag how great their company is to their friends.
  They take pride in what they do and who they work for, and they trust their organization.
- **Level 5: Growing as a Person.** Generation Y sees themselves as a proud employee who is—not only gaining monetary compensation for their work but also becoming a better person emotionally, mentally, or physically. At this level, they think, "Working at Company X has actually helped me become a better person."

It is your job as manager to help them reach that highest level, where in addition to receiving a paycheck, they are also able to make a difference and, at the same time, become a better person because of your leadership.

Work as Fun

Generation Y is one of the most educated generations in history. They grew up with teachers and TV shows that made learning fun, such as *Sesame Street* and *Mr. Rogers.*

Explore different ways to have fun at work. Here are some ideas:

- Every month, have dress-up day, where employees set the theme.
- Play short videos clips of 10 to 20 minutes in the break room (TED.com).
- Before a meeting, play someone's favorite music from an iPod brought in by a coworker.
- Suggest bringing in foods from around the world. (Generation Y enjoys discovering new foods.)
- Start an office Olympics. For example, have a paper clip flip toss or see how fast somebody can respond to an e-mail.
- Vote on company shirts designed by the employees. Just get creative.

Good Communication

Generation Y workers like feedback. In fact, they thrive on it. One reason is because they are a Nintendo Generation, used to having immediate feedback and seeing how well they performed (based on what level they have reached and what their score is).

Provide feedback in a timely manner and frequently; they want to know how they are doing *right now*. Giving feedback monthly or annually is not frequent enough. If they feel they are not doing well or that the boss doesn't like them, they will probably start to look for a job elsewhere.

A few quick and easy ways to give feedback are to stop workers in the hallway and say thank you, praise them in a meeting, leave notes on their desks, or send e-mails or text messages. Communication is about connecting with someone, and can come in the form of receiving a complimentary text for a job well done.

If you want to connect with Generation Y, learn how to text. Most young people will gladly donate their time to show you how to text, because now you're entering into their world of communication—and being able to send out a text message along with an e-mail shows that you can relate to them.

Generation Y and Loyalty

Some people think that Generation Y is not as loyal as some others. However, they are a "see it to believe it" generation, and if you can demonstrate loyalty consistently, they will return that to you and your organization.

Generations like the Baby Boomers and Gen-Xers grew up with the idea that loyalty was just given, where you gave a company 15, 20, or 30 years and they took care of you.

Generation Y grew up doing case studies in colleges and reading examples of how companies mismanaged people's money or how a company was there one day and gone the next. They saw family financial fortunes dwindle to near-nothing due to mismanaged funds, or they saw their parents get laid off after working for a company for 20 or 30 years.

Generation Y can be loyal, but they will not simply follow along blindly like previous generations.

Seven Ways Generation Y Improves the Workforce

Generation Y improves the workforce in several ways:

1. **They are very tech savvy.** They like technology and have an incredible ability to learn about it. They can have a new iPhone today and quickly learn how to use the latest iPhone two years from now.
2. **They also improve the workforce by their ability to change and adapt.** They are not hard set in their ways and rapidly deal with change to make a product or service better.
3. **They improve the workforce by their desire to get things done today, *right now*, and they are very speed-driven.** For example, they go to Google when they want certain information, and within their search, they usually find their answers within minutes. Speed is very important in business today, especially with the rise of global competition.

4. **They have high levels of confidence.** The workforce benefits from their confidence, a number one ingredient of an outstanding salesperson.

5. **They are expert multitaskers.** This generation grew up watching *The Simpsons,* eating their macaroni and cheese, and instant messaging their friends online all at the same time. This ability serves them well in the work environment.

6. **They are direct.** They have the ability to straight talk, to tell you what is on their mind, to be direct and to tell you what they feel. Their authenticity is beginning to dilute the political correctness and the political games that go on in modern organizations.

7. **They are health and environmentally conscious**. They are interested in eating healthy and staying active. They also care about the environment; this is a generation of people who grew up recycling.

PART

3 | Productivity

8

Prioritize for Productivity

Y ou are the CEO of your life, the chief effectiveness officer. How you spend your time, how you delegate, plan, organize, and deal with interruptions is all up to you. You are responsible for being productive. I identify four corners of productivity to help you achieve the best decisions for your business.

Four Corners of Productivity

Time	Plan
Focus	Delegate

1. Know where your time is going.
2. Plan the day before.
3. Focus on high-payoff items.
4. Delegate for results and not the process.

Let's start with the first corner. How do you spend your *time,* and what do you actually accomplish in a day? More often than not, the day can get away from you and go something like this:

You go to work, read a newspaper, jump on the computer, and read and respond to some e-mails. Then a colleague walks in and says, "Hey, it's time to go to lunch." You look at your watch and think, "Where has the time gone, and what did I get done?"

A great way to chart your time is to divide your day into two parts: (1) the time you walk in until lunchtime and (2) lunchtime until you leave.

Let's say your typical workday is 9 to 5. You begin at 9 AM and stop for lunch at noon. Just before breaking for lunch, write down what you actually accomplished from 9 AM till noon. That is the first part of your day. Then after you return and work from 1 PM to 5 PM, just before leaving for home, write down what you accomplished during the afternoon.

Charting your time allows you to identify when you are at your best, that is, when you are able to get the most done. This is referred to as your peak time. Not only does this time-keeping method help you identify your peak time, but it also allows you to identify some time wasters.

The second corner of productivity is to *plan* the day before. Preparation begets confidence, and the more you prepare and plan your day ahead of time, the more flexible you can be as unexpected tasks arise throughout the day. Planning while you are on the way to work can make for a stressful day.

Leadership Tip

A successful day starts the day before with planning. A stressful day starts as you drive into work and plan.

Does this scenario sound familiar? While driving to work, or taking that regular 20-minute train commute, you mentally plan all you'll get done that day, thinking you've got the world's greatest plan. Upon arriving at work, you quickly discover that your boss wants you to work on another project. You end up dealing with what seem like 30,000 interruptions and find yourself in a very chaotic, panicky, and stressed-out state.

Planning your work schedule the day before enables you to make adjustments when the unexpected occurs. It also reduces overall stress from those unexpected events.

The third corner of productivity is to *focus* on high-payoff items. What actions do you actually perform, and what results do you accomplish during your day? What do you work on of real value to you and your organization? Activity doesn't necessarily lead to productivity. Be concerned with the actual goal-oriented results you accomplish rather than the number of hours a day or week you work.

The last corner of productivity is to *delegate* for results and not the process. For example, if you went to Brandon, Florida, on a Thursday and stopped by my friend's parents' house, you would find them making 50 peanut butter and jelly sandwiches for the homeless, like they do every Thursday. But they wouldn't be making them together.

I have great respect for my friend's dad. He's one of my mentors and a role model in my life. However, when it comes to delegation, he delegates the process and not the results.

Let's say you arrive there, find him making sandwiches and offer to help. You start talking and everything is great, until it comes time to make the sandwiches, and he gives you the role of spreading the peanut butter. He prefers to deal with the jelly because he whips it, which makes it easier to spread.

Now it's time to spread the peanut butter on the bread for the sandwiches, and he's working on his jelly. He might take a step back, look at you and say, "Oh . . . is that how you do it?"

Being the nice person you are, you say, "Well, how would you like me to do it?"

And he might say something like, "Well, that's not how I would do it. Let me show you how I would do it." And then he shows you how to spread peanut butter on a piece of bread.

You do it his way, and after about 10 minutes he says, "Well, that's not how I would do it. Let me show you again. Weren't you paying attention last time?"

During the process of making peanut butter sandwiches, you are either discouraged and want to give up or trying to conform to his way and his process. This is an example of delegating the process, that is, forcing someone to follow your process. It makes for a very stressful environment and is also counterproductive.

Delegating for results is a bit different. A critical part of it is to inspect what you expect. For example, say my buddy Nathan and I decide to make sandwiches for the needy. I turn to him and say, "Nathan, make this sandwich as if you were going to eat it."

I don't care what he spreads the peanut butter with—a spoon, a folk, a spatula, a knife, it doesn't matter. After I see the first one and it looks great, I'm going to let him go. That is delegating for results and not the process.

Stop Trying to Be Superman

One reason we fall short on delegation is because we want to do it ourselves and think that no one can do a better job than we can. For example, Superman flies around the world and saves everyone who's in danger. But when Superman is in danger for his life, who saves him? Nobody. He must save himself. Stop trying to be Superman and ask for help.

A friend who owns his own business always gets on my case for not doing my own website development. He says, "Eric, it's so easy; you can do it." He does his own, but my expertise is not in website development, nor is his.

When I say he needs an expert to help him with delegation, at the end of the day he says, "Eric, you can save money by doing it, and you can do it on your own." When you compare his website to mine, it's obvious that he does it himself and that I use a professional. You have to know what you are good at and when to ask for help.

Why To-Do Lists Don't Work?

Many people use to-do lists but frequently find themselves frustrated with them. One reason they don't work well is that people put an inordinate amount of items on them, on average anywhere from 12 to 15 items. The problem is that if you keep a to-do list, you try to accomplish 12 to 15 items every single day.

You go to work feeling pretty good, have your favorite cup of coffee, and think everything is going great—until you see those 12 to 15 items. Instantly, you feel overwhelmed, depressed, or defeated even before you start your day. You may tell yourself you can get it all done, and then ultimately accomplish only three of the items. But at the end of the day, you leave without completing the list, and tomorrow's list is still in front of you.

It's human nature to focus on what we leave undone and to leave work feeling overwhelmed and stressed, thinking, "Man, I'll never get it all done!"

Leadership Tip

One of the fastest ways to burn out at work is to place unrealistic expectations on yourself.

This is one of the reasons I don't like to-do lists. Another is that we tend to start with the easiest items, thinking we have time to complete all or most of them. "I've got to go ask Jan in accounting a question on a particular invoice." And while you're there, you find yourself talking about topics such as the previous night's episode of *American Idol*. Then 30 minutes of unproductive time pass.

Another reason I don't like to-do lists is because many have no time limit. Those 12 to 15 items you laid out don't tell you in parentheses how much time it takes to complete each item.

Running Lists—Papp's Priority List

Instead of doing a to-do list, I like to have a running list that contains everything you think about doing or want to accomplish. It usually has anywhere from 20 to 30 items. Put everything you need to get done on your running list. And here's a tip: when you think it, ink it. Just get it out of your head and put it on your running list.

Then every day transfer those items from your running list to a Papp's priority list. (Yes, that is Papp's as in my last name. No, it's not Pabst as in beer, which will leave you with a nasty hangover in the morning.) A Papp's priority list will help you to become more productive.

Pick four items from your running list and transfer them to your Papp's priority list. Now you have to think to prioritize, whereas on the to-do list you just had a long list of items.

Next to each item write down how long it will take you to complete that item. Just take a guess; for example, 31 minutes to 65 minutes. When you add up the time for those four items, they should total no more than 3 to 4 hours, because you have to account for interruptions, such as phone calls, people coming into your office, e-mails, and spur-of-the-moment meetings.

I read in a study that the average person goes to work for 8.5 hours a day, but the average person works for only 4.5 hours a day. So having a priority list of 3 to 4 hours' of work to complete will help you accomplish more realistic daily goals.

Decide what you want, decide what you are willing to exchange for it. Establish your priorities and go to work.

—H. L. Hunt

Seven Ways to Increase Productivity

Now let's look at seven ways to increase productivity at work and at home:

1. **Purge unused or seldom used items daily.** It's amazing that 20 to 25 years ago there was no such thing as storage. Now it seems I can't even go three to five blocks without seeing some type of storage or utility place. There are cold storage, indoor and outdoor storage, and all types of storage places popping up everywhere, and it is a multimillion-dollar business.

   The people making money are those who capitalize on the fact that Americans are pack rats. We like to hold on to things, like a collection of *National Geographic* magazines, even though it's worth nothing. There is even a cable TV show called *Hoarders* that addresses this topic. Holding on to things we don't really need chokes our productivity.

   That's why I say to purge daily and get in the habit of purging. If you don't need something, are not going to use it, or haven't used something in three to six months, just throw it away or donate it.

   People who say, "Oh, just in case I need it," hang on to items unnecessarily. But that action (or inaction) prevents them from being productive. Get in the habit of purging daily by letting go of stuff and throwing it away. You'll feel so much better and so much more relieved. And you'll be able to get more done and be more productive.

2. **Slow down and relax.** I'm amazed when I'm around people who have achieved a great amount of success. It's almost like they have time. They don't check their watches, aren't on a tight time frame, and have time to give. It just seems that they truly have a sense of inner peace.

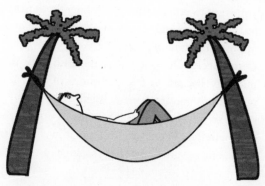

When you talk to people nowadays, they say, "Oh, I'm crazy busy; I'm swamped," like those are the hip or cool things to say. But the fact is, slowing down can actually increase your productivity by allowing you to work in a calm and goal-focused manner.

Ask yourself: "What am I doing? Am I very productive? What am I working on? What am I working toward? What is this all for?"

No matter how much you accomplish in life, if you don't have inner peace, you still will not feel productive. I talk more about this in Chapter 11.

3. **Use calendars.** The third way to increase productivity is to have a *monthly calendar* on your desk and a yearly calendar on your wall, because they help you to see the big picture. A desk calendar helps you stay more focused, because you can see three or seven months down the road. And both put you in the mind-set of planning ahead and being more productive with your time.

4. **Use dry erase boards.** The fourth way to be productive is to use *dry erase boards* to help you focus on written monthly goals by giving top-of-mind awareness as you look at them daily. When your boss asks what you are working on, you can point to it and say, "That's exactly what I'm working on." Try to keep the total number of goals to three to four to avoid overload.

5. **Ask for help.** Two of my favorite quotes are "No man is an island" and "Ask for help not because you're weak but because you want to remain strong." Asking for help can shorten your learning curve and save you a lot of time and frustration as opposed to going it alone.

6. **Outsource.** Outsourcing is the fifth way to increase productivity because it frees up more of your time. In a great book by Timothy Ferriss called *The 4-Hour Workweek*, he talks extensively about the benefits of outsourcing to enhance productivity. There are also great websites that offer services on a variety of topics, such as managing e-mails,

conducting research, or helping you in any business capacity. Three examples are www.odesk.com, www.elance.com, and www.fiverr.com. A majority of the illustrations in this book came from Fiverr.com.

7. **Have a productive mind-set.** Finally, have a *productive mind-set.* When you run an errand, maximize it. For example, before going to Jan's desk in human resources, look around your desk. "What should I take? Jan is on the third floor, and I can also drop these folders off in the conference room and return this report to Michael on second."

   When shopping, before you go into a store to buy something, know exactly what you want to buy and the location in the store. Have that in mind so that you spend only 15 minutes shopping, as opposed to 50 minutes.

Four Ways to Get Organized

I've found four ways to help me stay better organized:

1. **Hire a professional organizer.** Either hire a professional organizer or ask someone you know who is a very good organizer to help you. Let's say you open your garage door, and bikes, weedwackers, rakes, and other items start pouring out.

   Then you see your neighbor Tom, who opens his garage door to reveal a garage with everything neatly laid out. He has put up a corkboard. His hammers are laid out. Anytime you go over to borrow something he says, "Oh sure, that's right here," because he knows exactly where everything is.

   If you're struggling to get organized, ask for help. "Tom, can you help me one Saturday, and I'll cut your grass for a couple of weeks?" He'll probably be more than willing to help you.

2. **Create a type of filing system.** Have a system for items, such as mail or documents, that land on your office desk. Create a system for them, like a filing system. A good book called *The E-Myth,* by Michael Gerber, is all about having systems to be successful in business.

3. **Put things back in their right place.** It's simple and you've heard it since kindergarten, but it is so true. Let's say you're at home and you pick out a shirt to wear. You put it on and think, "This shirt doesn't really go with my pants." So you take the shirt off, and instead of hanging it up neatly in your closet, you toss it over your bedpost.

   How long will it take for that shirt on your bedpost to get back into the closet? Probably about a week, and it may even require someone else putting it back for you.

   Get in the habit of putting things back where they belong, because not putting things back in their rightful place usually takes two to three times longer to actually get there.

4. **Have a clean desk.** Having a clean desk is almost like having a clear mind-set to operate. It reinforces the idea that less is actually more, and it keeps you focused on what you want to accomplish.

E-mail, How Important Is It . . . Really?

Over time, I've discovered some great tips about e-mail, including ways to increase productivity and become better organized:

1. When you start your day, *don't start it by checking your e-mail*. Instead, begin with a task on your Papp's priority list. People who start their day checking their e-mail usually check it anywhere from 40 to 50 times a day. So begin with a task and check your e-mail later, after you've worked awhile.

   Checking your e-mail every time you get one actually lowers your productivity and, makes it more difficult to focus.

Leadership Tip

The less frequently you check your e-mail, the more productive day you'll have.

2. A great tip is to *process several messages at a time* instead of answering just one response, and do that for about 20 minutes.

3. *Purge e-mails* and see if you can delete them constantly. This will avoid that friendly reminder from IT folks saying, "Please delete your inbox; your inbox is exceeding storage and your account will be shut off in seven days if you don't." As you purge, you may even find valuable e-mails, whether from an old friend you never replied to or from a potential new client.

4. *Keep your messages short* and to the point. Bullet points or numbered lists are terrific. When I receive e-mails that are so long that I have to scroll down to see the complete message, my first reaction is to close the e-mail, saving it for review later. Very few people have time for long e-mails, so if you have a lengthy message to convey, send the bulk of the information as an e-mail attachment that the recipient can easily print it off.

5. You jeopardize your *e-mail credibility* when you start sending too many e-mails. Let's say you work for a company and the president just discovered e-mail. He sends one e-mail that everyone opens immediately (he *is* the president). Then he sends out another e-mail, which everyone also opens. But if he sends out several e-mails every day or even every week, his e-mail credibility goes down and you may not open the next e-mail as promptly.

6. *Don't send e-mails when you're upset.* E-mails last longer than emotions. So when something is very heated or emotional to talk about, don't talk about it in an e-mail. If you're upset and someone writes to you in a tone that irritates you; take time to cool down and regain control of your emotions. What you say in an e-mail can last a lot longer than the initial emotion you had for that particular situation.

7. *Send cc's and Reply to All e-mails only when necessary.* Of the useless e-mails that people receive every day, probably 20 to 30 percent are cc and Reply to All messages that the recipient didn't need to be included on.

Ask yourself: "Am I going to cc someone that I just want to keep in the loop, or do they really need to be in the loop? Am I hitting Reply to All because I just want everyone to know what I'm doing, or is it really that important?"

Defeating Procrastination

My definition of procrastination is to put off something that should have been done a week, month, or year ago. We live in a nation of procrastination, seemingly believing that we can just put it off and put it off and get it done at the last minute. But there are ways to overcome procrastination. Interview someone in your office who has already completed the same type of project you are working on. This gives you confidence, because you say to yourself, "If she can do it, then I can do it," and you can see the system the other person used.

If you struggle with writing a proposal, ask a coworker who already wrote a proposal to that same client for his help. Buy him lunch and interview him. If he did it, then you can do it.

Apply the *20-minute rule*. Just working on a project 20 minutes at a time can help you get started and gain the momentum needed to actually accomplish what you want to accomplish. As Rocky Balboa said in *Rocky*, "It ain't so bad." You're just doing 20 minutes at a time, and it's not that painful.

I used to work as a personal trainer, and when people would come in for their first session, I would usually train them for 45 to 60 minutes. And what I found is that people weren't coming back. And I needed to figure out why.

The answer was simple: I was working them too hard, and they couldn't come back. So I changed my game plan and started using 20-minute workouts for the initial training. Clients started coming back for additional sessions. The next thing I knew, 20 minutes increased to 30 minutes, and then 30 minutes grew to 50 minutes. And that was the whole idea, just doing it little by little.

You can apply this rule, too, even if you need to go to a store and buy a stopwatch. Just click on that stopwatch and dive into your project 20 minutes. Applying the 20 minute. rule can help you start and finish projects you are procrastinating.

Procrastinating a project can cause you more pain long term as opposed to taking action and completing it. Two types of pain are the *pain of discipline* and the *pain of regret*. Let's say you want to get in shape for your 20-year high school reunion. The discipline is that you prepare by working out daily, eating healthy, and making sure to get proper rest.

The pain of regret is that it's now time for the reunion, and you haven't done anything. Now you feel regret and find yourself saying "should have/could have" a lot. "Oh, I wish I could have . . ." "Oh, I should have . . ." Usually, the regret is more painful than the discipline.

Just jump in and do something, even if you don't know where to start. When you jump in on a project, you'll find that you actually do it. And just that act of momentum helps you begin to accomplish something.

Dealing with Interruptions

Has someone ever come into your office and said, "Hey, you gotta minute?" Don't reply, "Yes," because 1 minute to that person could be 1 minute or it could be 20 minutes—it may even be 1 hour. Have the person be specific, defining how much of your time is needed.

The language you use when you are interrupted is very important. If your time is very limited, say something like, "I've got 3 minutes now or 15 minutes later. Which do you prefer?"

What you are saying is, "If you can spit it out to me in 3 minutes, I'm all ears. But if not and it's going to require more time, then let's talk about it later."

If you have no time at all, say something like, "To better serve you, I can come to your office between 2:00 and 2:15, or 3:00 and 3:15." Or, "For me to better listen to you, I can meet you at (whatever time works best for both of you)."

If that person wants or needs more of your time, like more than 3 minutes, always go to his or her office and always schedule it after lunch.

One reason you always go to the other person's office is because that gives you the option of leaving. You are in control. If the person comes to your office and sits down, the next thing you know, 20 or 30 minutes go by and you think, "How am I going to get this person out of my office?"

A reason you always schedule it after lunch and postpone it for later in the day is because one of three things usually happens:

1. The person solves his or her own problem.
2. The person seeks assistance from someone else (someone who doesn't handle interruptions well).
3. It's really not that big of a deal and you show up, and they say not to worry about it.

Another way of dealing with interruptions is to keep your business posture. When someone comes through your doorway or enters your cubicle and interrupts you, make sure you still have your hands on your keyboard or your pen in hand, like you're working on something, and just glance up at them.

You can say something like, "How can I help you?"

This still shows your business posture. But the minute you kick back, put your hands over your head, or push back from your desk, you signal to the other person, "Hey, stay awhile. Come on in. Let's talk about it. Kick up your feet."

You must always let others know that your time is valuable. If you don't, then it's not valuable to them, and they will interrupt you for anything.

Another way to deal with interruptions is to shut your door. Sometimes you just need to shut your door for time to work on your tasks. I believe that the person who invented the open-door policy is probably out of business or very unproductive, because people will abuse an open-door policy.

Effective Meetings

Corporations, organizations, and associations waste a lot of time every year with unproductive meetings. Before you have a meeting, make sure you have a purpose. What's the reason for the meeting? Is it because it's just "scheduled," or do you have a definite purpose? When you have a meeting, make sure that some decision or commitment comes out of it.

Effective meetings encourage healthy conflict (also discussed in Chapter 5). With healthy conflict, people share their ideas and opinions, debate and give feedback, and become truly invested in the topics. This is critical for productive meetings. Otherwise, you find yourself chairing a meeting where you do 80 percent of the talking. Then when people leave, they don't understand your point or why you went down a particular road.

Boring Meeting = Bad Results

Have you ever heard a chief executive officer (CEO) conclude a staff presentation with, "Would anyone like to add anything?"

Everyone just sits there and smiles politely as if saying, "Yes, we completely agree with you, and we are too afraid of speaking our mind for fear of repercussion."

As a leader, one of your goals is to foster an environment where healthy conflict exists. Your organization is paying people for their service and intellectual capital. I don't know if we forget to think and brainstorm, or if the situation doesn't lend itself to that type of behavior.

Three ways that you can foster a healthy meeting environment follow:

1. **Remove your ego.** Who cares if someone comes up with a better idea than yours? Use it. Be humble. Use some self-deprecating humor to put your staff at ease while still maintaining your authority.
2. **Present results not history**. Be careful of how much emphasis you put on sayings like, "We've never done that before; that's the way we've always done it." If you are results-focused, usually the best practices will appear.
3. **Share the victory and own the defeat**. Your people will respect you so much more and be more committed on future projects. When people demonstrate accountability, you can't help but look internally to see what can be improved.

One last note on meetings: start and end them on time. Think of the message you send if you constantly start meetings 10 to 15 minutes late to wait for stragglers to arrive. The message you send to those who arrive on time is that you are rewarding those who show up late, because they are the ones you are waiting for. Make sure the messages you send are very clear. You punish them by keeping them later on when they were the ones who showed up early and on-time.

Likewise, ending meetings on time says to your audience, "Your time is valuable, and I'm going to keep this to the time allotted."

9

Fourth Quarter Living Decision Making

What's It All About?

What is it all about for you? Have you ever asked yourself that question? Have you ever asked yourself what you're working for? Obviously, you're working to pay the rent and other bills, but at the same time, what does your life consist of?

A speaker once asked his audience, "What are you running toward, and what are you running from?" That caused me to stop and think about doing things on purpose without being caught up in society norms. Too often we seem to get caught up in the rat race of trying to keep up with the Joneses, or we work late because that's what everybody else is doing. But we don't ask ourselves what it's really all about.

A friend recently told me that she had changed her whole lifestyle, her personal and professional life, and how she went about work. And this all happened because one day, she asked herself, "Am I living or just existing?" She felt she was just existing, so she made significant changes.

When we get to the fourth quarter of life, we begin to see that: "Maybe I should spend more time here. Maybe I need to adjust my priorities here. Maybe I was too focused on this. I really wish I had done that."

If you find yourself caught up in the rat race or in some web of society, don't wait until the fourth quarter of life to start making important decisions. Start by asking yourself what your life is all about and then set good priorities in order to make good decisions.

Importance of a Vision

What is your vision for yourself and your family? Where do you see yourself 5 and 10 years from now? What do you see yourself doing, and what is your lifestyle like?

When someone says "vision," we often think of a company or an organization. But have your own vision to see where you are going and if you are headed in the right direction. Your vision, or lack of a vision, is carried out daily, so make sure you have a game plan and are working toward something.

One of the most widely sold books in history, the Bible (Proverbs 29:18) says, "Where there is no vision, the people perish."

Driving across country to visit relatives in another state, you have a map, a GPS system, a route, and a plan. But if you leave home without a plan, no direction, and no guidance, chances are, you will not reach your destination—or if you do, it will take you much longer.

Decisions for Today, Tomorrow, and in 50 Years

Fourth quarter decision making is having the ability to see 10 to 20, and in some cases even 50 years, down the road. I recently heard Tom Monaghan, the founder of Domino's Pizza in the 1960s and previous owner of the Detroit Tigers, give a speech. His latest project, Ave Maria University in South Florida, is one of the most closely watched Catholic universities in the country, with the potential to affect millions of lives.

As one of the founders, Mr. Monaghan is able to calculate far into the future, and his vision is very impressive. He shared with us his 70-year vision for Ave Maria University: "I believe we will have 4,000 faithful priests, some of whom will already become bishops. We will have 2,500 sisters; many will be teaching in Catholic schools around the country. By 2078, we will have trained some 12,000 Catholic teachers and 1,500 principals."

Having this type of vision allows you to reach your goals. We need to apply this technique to our lives and ask where we see ourselves years in the future. Ask yourself, "What is the legacy that I will leave?"

Shared Vision

A shared vision in an organization encourages collaboration and fosters an environment of engagement. It grants a high level of ownership for employees. Having a shared vision is the hope to get you through uncertain times. People are more likely to be committed to the outcome and success of their organization when they believe in the direction. Shared vision in its simplest form is having everyone on the same page, having a clear focused direction.

Make a Decision; Be Decisive

In modern society, people are sometimes afraid to make decisions and take a course of action, as though we've become a society of fence-sitters. "Oh, I don't know if I can do that. I'll see. What happens if we fail? What happens if we look bad?"

Take the initiative and make a decision. If you make a mistake, so what?

A young intern once asked a famous IBM executive, "How do I increase my chances of success?" And the reply was, "Double your failure rate." You are able to do that only by taking action.

Fourth quarter decision making is about the ability to make a decision and execute. I once read that an idea is great, but an "I did it!" is even better.

If you have ever visited a retirement home or spent time with senior citizens, you probably never heard them talk about what they wouldn't do if they had it to do over again. Rather, they usually tell you what they should have done. Looking back, they wish they had either made more decisions or taken more action.

Right now, start thinking about what you want to do. Don't wait until the fourth quarter of your life, when maybe you're in a retirement home, to say, "I wish I could have done this; I should have done that."

At the age of 15, John Goddard wrote down 127 goals, and to this day he has accomplished 109 of them. They include climbing mountains and going on extreme river adventures.

Two years ago, a family friend named Martin talked to my parents about retirement and how he loved to travel. He told them that after he retired, he planned to travel. My dad urged him to start traveling right then, but he didn't. Unfortunately, a few months later our friend passed away. He waited until it was too late to realize his goals. This doesn't need to happen to you. You can begin now to make decisions that fulfill your life.

Short-Term Gain, Long-Term Pain

Frequently when people are hasty in the decision-making process and make quick decisions, they realize a short-term gain but experience long-term pain. Fourth quarter decision making is about having the wisdom and the knowledge to make a decision that is not only important for today but that also will impact the future.

Decisions are not just for a short-term, small-term gain, but also for long-term gain. All too often the economy falls because people make financial decisions based on the short term. In trying to make a quick buck (short-term gain), they ultimately end up in financial trouble and suffer long-term pain.

Epitaph Exam

Two things are guaranteed in life. One is that you will have to pay taxes, and two is that you will die. Anything you do in between is up to you. It's something to think about.

How do you want to be remembered? Let's say it's your funeral and people have come to pay their last respects. What are they saying about you? How do they describe you? Do they say you were a good person who strove to help others?

If you died today, what kind of legacy would you leave behind? What do you want people to say? How do you want people to remember you?

Fourth quarter living is about creating the life you want to live right now and living your life as a good example for others. The good news is that you can begin now to be that example for others, to be that person of service.

Sometimes people wait until they get too old to leave a positive legacy, so start creating your legacy now to have a positive impact on people's lives, because you never know when a day will be your last day.

Fourth Quarter Football

If you have ever watched a football game or played football, you know players have a tendency in the fourth quarter to hold up four fingers to indicate the start of the fourth quarter. But it also means that this is it. "This is the last quarter, and we're going into a situation where we must give it our all and put everything on the line."

You don't have to wait until the fourth quarter of life to start living and give all that you have to give to your own life and those around you. You can embrace that same football fourth quarter mentality right now and put it all on the line and live life to the fullest.

Personal Mission Statement

Fourth quarter living is about having a personal mission statement. If someone approached you and asked, "What are you living for?" What would you say? What is your personal mission statement?

I've thought about that and what I do as a speaker and trainer. My personal mission statement is to serve others through my gifts of listening and speaking. Maybe your mission statement is to be the best dad or the best mom possible. Or maybe "to develop the minds of the next generation." Or even "to build a healthier America." Think about it and examine what services you can contribute to society, where you actually serve others through your gifts and talents.

Taking Care of Yourself

Fourth quarter living and decision making means being in or working toward good physical health. Unfortunately, I see people in the fourth quarter of life with poor health. Some are able to turn their lives around and make adjustments, but for others it is too late. Don't wait until it's too late.

Begin living a healthful lifestyle now and focus on taking care of your body. Change your eating habits, become more physically active, or get more rest. The body is a temple that provides energy to do everything possible, so examine what you consume. We live in one of the largest and most obese countries in the world today, where food surrounds us and is accessible 24/7. The reality is that some of us need to exercise self-discipline and to have the mind-set of keeping a healthy body.

Learning from Our Mistakes

Fourth quarter living and decision making means being able to look back and learn from your mistakes and where you come from, to see what has and hasn't worked in the past.

The definition of *insanity* is doing the same thing over and over again and expecting a different result. Consider what is working and what's not working in your life. Ask yourself: "What areas in my life do I need to improve? What relationships do I need to patch up? What mistakes do I need to avoid and correct?"

10

The Power of Focus

What Are You Burning?

When I was eight years old, I remember going to my friend Nathan's house and playing outside with his mom's magnifying glass, scouring the yard for leaves. We gathered a nice pile and took it to the pavement, and then put the magnifying glass over the leaves. Within a couple of minutes, the power of the sun's rays coming together in a concentrated spot burned a hole right through the leaves.

That was one of the first times I actually experienced the power of focus, converging the energy of sunrays and being able to burn something. I remember thinking, "Wow! That's focus."

What are you burning in your life, both at work and at home? What are your goals? What areas do you focus on, and what do you want to accomplish?

Focus and Food

A husband and wife are deciding where they want to go for dinner and the wife asks, "Honey, where do you want to go for dinner tonight?"

The husband replies, "Oh, I don't know; just pick something."

The wife replies with, "How about Chinese?"

"Ooh, Chinese? You know, I just had that yesterday for lunch. Pick something else."

"Well, how about Italian?"

The husband says, "Ooh, Italian. I'm really trying to watch my carbohydrate intake."

This continues until somebody is eating leftovers or until somebody just picks a place, and either way, there's likely very little dinner conversation.

Most people are better at telling you what they don't want rather than telling you what they do want. It illustrates the power of focus and being able to figure out what it is you want. What do you really want in life?

137

Unfocused Behavior

I don't know the key to success, but the key to failure is trying to please everyone.

—Bill Cosby

What does unfocused behavior mean, and what does it look like? It can take on several forms. One form is to lack a system. Without a system, when you begin something, you kind of haphazardly do it.

Unfocused behavior may be having a strong need for approval and constantly seeking the approval of others. This may be a subconscious need rather than having an overt awareness. For example, instead of focusing on doing the work, a person constantly searches for praise or recognition for what he or she tries to do.

Unfocused behavior can also be having a need to make every decision, to sit in on every conference call, or to be present in every meeting. This often results in a lack of concentration on doing the work.

Unfocused Activities

- Checking your e-mail or text message every time you get one
- Checking your e-mail as your first activity of the day
- Not having a priority list for the day (just showing up with no plan)
- Being interrupted more frequently than what is necessary
- Talking 20 minutes when 2 minutes will do
- Having an overwhelming list of tasks to complete

Have you ever thought of what causes you to lose time? Just what or who is taking some or most of your time these days?

Take a minute and look around you right now. Is it your cell phone? Is it the constant texting and interruptions from your cell phone? Do you constantly need to check the e-mails on your cell phone? Are you constantly playing the games?

Take a look at the people you associate with, the social groups you belong to, and your friends. Some friends can be very time draining.

Can't Do It All

Have you ever talked to someone who seems to be engaged in everything: "Oh, I'm doing this, and I'm a part of this club, and on the weekends I go to this, and I belong to this church; and I'm actually pursuing my real estate license, and when the market turns around, I'm going to go back and become a realtor, and I'm also working on my MBA."

People like this give the impression that they are doing a lot, but in reality, they are doing a whole lot of nothing. They are trying to do too much. And the simple truth is that no one can do it all.

As a student at the University of Notre Dame, I once attended a club activities night in the Joyce Center. I was excited as I made my way around, seeing all of the clubs represented there. I thought: "Man, I want to be part of this club. I want to be part of the newspaper. I want to be part of the boxing team. I want to be part of the entrepreneur club."

Well, that lasted for about a week. It was simply too much to tackle and I couldn't keep up with all the different clubs and my academics. Anytime you try to do too much, you end up doing nothing. Trying to do it all is just another form of unfocused behavior. As one of my mentors says, "Move three things a mile rather than a hundred things an inch."

Daily Focus

Having a focus on daily activities comes under four areas of how you spend your day and your time, whether at work or at home.

I modified my concept based on Stephen Covey's four quadrants in his book, *The 7 Habits of Highly Successful People*. Let's consider each section:

Reactive Mode	**Proactive Mode**
Interruptions	**Time Wasters**

Being in the *reactive mode* means operating in a crisis mode, where everything becomes a priority. You may be in reactive mode because it is the nature of your job and what you do. Maybe you are in customer service, for example, and although you try to get caught up, you constantly feel like you're behind the eight ball. There is always stuff on your desk, you are always bogged down by the day-to-day activities, and you just keep putting things off because you have no help.

When in the *proactive mode*, not everything is a priority. Your priorities are clearly organized, and you know exactly what you are focused on and what you want to accomplish in your daily, weekly, and monthly goals.

Here's an example of the difference between reactive mode and proactive mode. I live in Tampa, Florida. I get in my car and drive to Jacksonville, Florida. I see that I have one-quarter tank of gas but keep going and think nothing of it.

The next thing I know I'm in traffic. Now the gas gauge is on E, and I hear that familiar little ding of the gas gauge! When I had one-quarter tank of gas, I could have made a proactive choice to stop and get gas. But I let it go and procrastinated. And because I procrastinated, I then found myself in a reactive, crisis mode. "Man! It's on E. I just heard the ding and saw the light." And now I'm scrambling around trying to get gas.

Being in a reactive state causes you to stress and become more anxious, and your anxiety level goes up, whereas being in the proactive state is less anxious. As much as possible, avoid putting yourself in a reactive, crisis mode.

Constant *interruptions* means exactly what it says. Your focus on performing any task is affected by interruptions. For example, if you ask a coworker what he completed that particular day, he might say, "Oh, I didn't get anything done." And frequently the reason for this is constant interruption—people coming and going and the phone constantly ringing.

Consider the nature of your job. If you are in customer service or customer support, interruptions are going to be a large part of your day. It's simply the nature and function of your job. Essentially, to be effective you must value your time, because when you value your time, others value it as well. So guard against spending a lot of your day with interruptions.

Time wasters really speaks for itself. Workplace examples include office chatter or office gossip, talking about what was on TV the night before, talking about fantasy football, or talking about sports. There are definitely times when you want to pull back and take a break, but make sure that a significant part of the day is not spent in time-wasting activities (definitely frowned upon by most bosses).

For a better outcome to your day, especially at work, concentrate on spending your time in a proactive state.

Focus and Technology

Technology is supposed to make our lives easier, and in many cases it does; for example, having a GPS system on your phone can quickly set you on the right path if you get lost on your way to a party. However, some people seem to become technology victims.

Frequently in my travels, I see people wearing a Bluetooth headset. (I like to call it the blinking cockroach.) And they seem so attached to it. Every time it goes off, it looks like they are talking to themselves. It's the same for people who have a BlackBerry, an iPhone, or a other smartphone.

I once read that 55 percent of people check their e-mail before they even get dressed in the morning. That's kind of a scary thought. Make sure that technology is working for you and that it helps you to keep your focus.

Parkinson's Law

Parkinson's Law states that *work expands to fill the time available to complete it.* Can you think back to the fifth grade when the teacher gave you three months to do a report? You probably could have done it in a week. But how long did you take? What were you doing the night before? Like most folks, you were probably writing the report.

But if the teacher said, "You've got three weeks to do this report," how long would it have taken you? Three weeks. The time that we allot for a project is usually the maximum amount of time we take to complete that project.

When you assign yourself a work project, it's very important to make sure that you don't assign yourself too much time. If you do, you risk filling it with something less important than the project at hand, and you also lose focus.

Just Say No!

In the late 1980s and early 1990s, First Lady Nancy Reagan championed the war against drugs and coined the popular theme with the phrase, "Just say no." I also say, "Just say no!"

A majority of the population has a hard time saying no to people, but it is impossible to always say yes to everyone and develop a keen sense of focus. People who say no usually have a good idea of their priorities and their focus.

People who say yes to everything and everyone usually develop some sort of pain later on, because they overcommit or overextend themselves. "Yes, I can be at that function. Yes, I can do this project." For a clearer focus of your goals, avoid saying yes to everything and everyone and just say no to situations that will distract you from your focus.

Creatures of Habits

A good habit can be hard to form and easy to break. A bad habit can be easy to form and hard to break. Whether or not you like change, we are all creatures of habit with the potential to develop good habits that help us maintain great focus. What habits do you perform daily that cause you to lose focus?

A potentially bad habit can be skipping breakfast. You find yourself eating a bigger lunch and feeling more fatigued and sleepy in the afternoon as a result.

A good habit I recommend is to start your day on the right foot by doing something for yourself, like going for a walk, meditating, or writing down your goals. And start with a fresh shower. Not only will you appreciate it and it wakes you up, but your colleagues will also benefit from this good habit as well.

Clarity Breeds Confidence

People who know what they want and work toward something are usually very confident individuals. Think, for example, of people who want to lose weight and know exactly how many pounds they want to lose and what they must do to reach their goals.

You can almost see the confidence in their eyes and hear the confidence in their tone of voice. They have clarity in the outcome they want and what they must do to achieve it.

This is true of anyone with a clear focus. When somebody says, "I'm going to become this, and this is how I'm going to get there," you see that person develop a sense of confidence, and that confidence stems from having clarity.

The clearer and more focused you are, the more your self-confidence will increase, and the more success you will have.

The 80/20 Rule

An eighteenth-century Italian economist named Vilfredo Pareto discovered that 80 percent of his country's wealth was controlled by 20 percent of the people. Using the 80/20 rule can help to determine ratios in your life to improve your focus.

For example, maybe 20 percent of the people you know cause 80 percent of your problems. Or 80 percent of your company's revenue comes from 20 percent of customers.

Consider this rule in your daily life with regard to your results, your efforts, and your problems.

Leadership Tip

The key in the 80/20 rule is knowing what activities yield the most return and what to focus on.

Examine the results and see what falls into the 80 percent category and what falls into the 20 percent category. Are your efforts obtaining the results you want?

Focus and Relationships

What are your criteria for a relationship? Knowing people well saves you from wasting time with those who bog you down with trivial matters. In your personal life, knowing whom you want to date is an initial step toward a good relationship.

In business, knowing what types of people you want to work with saves you from wasting time and sets the stage for success. Not knowing these dynamics wastes your time and potentially costs you revenue. The better you know your database, the more efficiently you can provide products and services to existing customers and potential clients.

For example, insurance and real estate agents can be much more effective if they know the types of clients in their business. Based on the 80/20 rule, it's really helpful to get rid of the 20 percent of clients causing them 80 percent of the problems.

The Hedgehog Concept

In his book *Good to Great,* Jim Collins talks about a hedgehog concept and the difference between a hedgehog and a fox. The fox is very sly and cunning, unfocused, and scattered, whereas the hedgehog is very focused and simplistic.

The author has "Three Circles" that I have modified to help you gain clarity in your business or life in general. Three questions from the book have helped me and I have modified them here:

1. What are you best at?
2. What do you do that is a high economic payoff for you or your organization?
3. What are you passionate about, and what really excites you?

It is my belief that when you combine all three circles, you not only collect a paycheck and earn an income, but you also start to make a difference and feel a sense of belonging and connection between your goals and objectives with the company.

How Long Did You Work?

Frankly, who cares? I'm amazed when folks talk to me about how many hours a week they work, or how many hours a day they put in, or that they put in all this time. It doesn't matter. Hard work alone does not equal results. It guarantees only that you are going to be tired. You have to work focused, and you have to work smart.

Don't worry about how much time someone puts in, whether they put in 20 hours or 50 hours. Don't be so caught up in, "If I work 10 hours today, then I'll work 15 hours tomorrow."

You don't hire people to punch a time clock or just to fill in time. You hire them to achieve a desired result. Always focus on the results. Make sure you know the desired result you want someone to achieve and see that the person actually achieves the goal.

Focus and Communication

The more focused your message is, the more it has an impact. The next time you facilitate a meeting, make two to three points that truly stand out in your presentation. You want people to come out of the meeting fully understanding the intent of your message.

In a hallway, when a person stops someone who attended your session and says, "Hey, you just went to Eric's session. What did he talk about?" The attendee can say, "He talked about these two points." And bam! They've got them. When you as the presenter are focused and deliver two to three points it makes it easier for audience members to share your message with others. So be very focused in your communication.

We see this concept with great speeches. On August 28, 1963, on the steps of the Lincoln Memorial, Martin Luther King, Jr., gave his famous "I Have a Dream" speech. Even if you don't know the rest of his speeches, you probably know this one, because he repeated that phrase over and over again: "I have a dream." He spoke about his dream for equality and a better America. Repetition helped him better focus and communicate his message and impart more clarity to his audience.

When communicating one on one or in a presentation, repeating your message over and over again helps add clarity and focus to any message, especially when accompanied by stories that illustrate the points you want to emphasize.

PART

4

Personal Development

11

Finding Strength in Silence

Leading with Silence

Where do leaders find their inspiration? Where do they go to jump-start the internal drive that promotes inner peace? The answer is in silence. We look at history and find leaders who faced tough times and difficult situations, like Martin Luther King, Jr., in his fight for civil rights during the 1960s. Where did he find his courage and the inspiration to write his famous "I Have a Dream" speech?

In India, where did Mahatma Gandhi find strength for peaceful protests in his country? In the United States, how did John F. Kennedy remain calm in the midst of an apocalyptic threat to world peace during the Cuban Missile Crisis? When England was under attack from her enemies, where did Winston Churchill find the strength and determination to win battles?

The answer is through silence. When we retreat to silence, we tap into the inner calm that allows us to search for answers. We find ideas strong enough to move a country and are able to formulate words that influence millions.

When Is Noise Too Much?

Finding silence in modern times can be very difficult, especially with the ever-present noise that surrounds us. Constant distractions compete for our attention, and we seem to go from one distraction to the next.

Advertisers fight for our attention on TV, on the radio, and even on iPods. We go to work and are bombarded with gossip and office chatter. Distraction is literally everywhere.

Even our cell phones have become somewhat of a "human LoJack." We need to put down the phone and curb distractions in order to think more clearly, because it has become increasingly difficult to go where people cannot gain access.

We see what constant noise does to our attention span and how it gets shorter every year. For example, if TV commercials fail to grab our attention within the first five seconds, we quickly find another channel to watch.

Try this self-test. See if you can sit in total silence for seven minutes, making no physical movements and focusing only on your breathing. Once you accomplish this, see if you can then start to slow down your thoughts. Try it and you will be amazed at how relaxed you can become.

The next time you walk into your local grocery or convenience store and you're in line at the checkout, look around to see what's there. You'll likely find energy drinks like 5-Hour Energy, Monster, and Red Bull. It seems that some sort of brand-new energy drink is out there giving us all the lifelong vitality we need, whether it's a triple shot of this or a double espresso of that.

But just what are we doing to ourselves? How much caffeine do we need? In many ways, we're quickly becoming an overstimulated society dependent on caffeine. We just go, go, go—and often don't know where we are going. We live in a society where we burn out early.

Recently, I was talking to a young upstart attorney in Los Angeles, California, who told me that she had gotten burned out on her job. When she told me she was only 27 years old, I asked her, "How did you get burned out at 27?"

She said, "I was constantly on the go. It was constantly go, go, go."

What good is living in an overstimulated society? We even subject our kids to this mentality, putting little Johnny or little Suzy in three different activities until they have no time for rest. We take them to baseball, ballet, soccer, or karate practice, and then put a TV in our car so they can be entertained and stimulated on the 10-minute commute to school.

It's time we start to shut out that type of exposure to our kids and ourselves.

The Art of Thinking

One of my favorite quotes comes from my mom: "Figure it out." When I was small, anytime I couldn't think of something or didn't know how to do something, she would always say to figure it out. And that always led me to think.

Thinking has almost become a lost art in our society; problem solving, creativity, curiosity, you name it—they are becoming uncommon skills. We don't even think anymore. We just go from one routine to the next, thinking that activity means productivity. And that couldn't be further from the truth.

Dr. Albert Schweitzer (1952 Noble Peace Prize winner) was once asked, "Doctor, what's wrong with men today?" Dr. Schweitzer was silent a moment and then said, "Men simply don't think."

And that's exactly right. Many men and women simply don't think. They get caught up in people, things, and events that detract from thinking.

In business we ask, "What did our business do last year? What did our competitors do?" Sometimes there is a tendency to be lazy and rest on last year's laurels. Rather than take the time to exercise our brain, be creative, and solve problems, we seek answers from somebody else.

Take the time to stop and think for a while; take time to sit on a park bench for 5 or 10 minutes and think about what you are doing and where you're headed.

Retreat and Reflect

The ability to relax and reflect on life is a key component of success and leadership, but for some people the idea of retreating is not a simple concept. Consider it from a perspective of giving your mind a vacation, a time to reflect and figure things out. Go for a walk or sit on a park bench and allow your mind to wander.

Just relax. Sit back. Count back from 25 to 1 and feel your body release tension. A key to a successful life is being able to retreat and surrender—and knowing the right time to take breaks.

When you retreat, your body physically slows down, but it can take awhile for your thoughts to slow down. It's an important process, because as you're able to regain a sense of calmness and reflection, your mind clears so that you can begin to ask yourself questions.

For example: "Why am I here? What is my contribution? What are my strengths? What am I working toward? What am I maybe running from? What drives me? What makes me feel fulfilled? What brings me joy?"

Questions like these can get you started, and then you can add others. Just sit back, observe, and reflect on your life to regain control.

Know Thyself; Gain Control

The ancient Greek philosopher Socrates was famous for the maxim, "Know thyself." When you ask a four-year-old, "What do you want to do with your life?" he can rattle off three or four different things instantly: a fireman, a doctor, a lawyer, a paramedic. . . . But when you ask an eighth grader the same question, he might reply with just one or two options. In high school, he might choose one item or not even have an answer.

What did that person really want to do as a kid? What did his inner child say? Unfortunately, with age we start to lose ourselves as society begins to form us, and we begin to lose ourselves a little bit each year as others tell us how we should live our lives.

I like to hike the Appalachian Trail. It's a great way to avoid distractions, because it's just people and nature. Spend time alone to find your inner child and discover your true gifts and talents.

In his book *Emotional Intelligence,* Daniel Goleman writes about how to keep emotions under control. Gaining emotional control through silence can be a fine balance, especially when people fly off the handle without provocation. They become so upset that they become emotionally hijacked. Maintain self-control by taking time for yourself; this will prevent your emotions from getting the best of you.

Carefree Time and Letting Go

What happened to carefree time, to sitting outside and doing nothing on Sundays, or to spending half the day engaged in leisurely activity? My brother brought this point to my attention.

I once thought that technology would make our lives easier, but for the most part it's just the opposite. We tend either to pile on more burdens or to put ourselves in constant agenda mode, and sometimes we transfer our agenda to our kids by overfilling their activities.

A great idea for carefree time is to take a half-day and do something you wouldn't normally do. Just get in the car and drive or go to a park, but don't take a watch or a phone. Spend carefree time with people you love and care about, and don't worry about getting back to your normal routine at a certain time. You'll find it frees your mind and relaxes your body.

I read Hale Dwoskin's *The Sedona Method,* and the concept about letting go really impressed me. Try this exercise. Pick up a pen, pencil, or marker; grab it physically in your hand, and tightly squeeze it as though it's something you're holding on to that is stressing you out.

Really squeeze it hard and ask yourself, "Can I see my hand opening up? Can I see myself letting go of this pen? Can I see myself putting this down? What would happen if I put down this pen?"

Maybe you wouldn't stress out if you learned to let go. Maybe you could get a great night's sleep. Maybe you could learn how to forgive and start living your life again.

When you enter your office or home garage, sometimes the physical nature of things can be overwhelming. What do you need to let go of to gain more clarity, be a better person, and reduce stress?

Dealing with Stress

Stress surrounds us daily, and we must examine how it affects us. My plan for dealing with stress is the 10-10-10 rule, a stress barometer that can be applied to most situations.

Stress generally falls into one of three categories, and this is where my 10-10-10 rule comes into play (10 minutes–10 hours–10 days).

First, ask yourself these questions: "Why am I stressing about this? Can I stop stressing about this? Is this a big deal? Am I creating stress somehow? Do I need to slow down?"

Next, ask yourself where your stress falls in each of these categories: "Is it going to matter 10 minutes from now? Is it going to matter 10 hours from now? Is it going to matter 10 days from now?"

Answering these questions puts stress in its proper place and reduces its impact on your day, your outlook, and your life.

To combat stress:

- **Enjoy the silence.** As we've discussed, taking time to enjoy silence helps reduce stress. You can enjoy the silence by riding home from work without music, going for a walk after dinner, or sitting in a chair with no distractions, no interruptions, no stimulation, and no noise.

- **Create a gratitude list.** What are you grateful for? Do you have a family and friends, a job, and a roof over your head? Do you have people who love you? Do you have goals? Do you have physical and mental health? Create a list and keep it either in your smartphone or by your bedpost. One of the best attitudes someone can have throughout life is to have an attitude of gratitude for all of his or her blessings.

- **Take naps.** It's amazing that Americans get such little sleep nowadays. Sleep is free, yet in today's fast-paced society, we are always trying to get so much more done. And for what, and at what cost?

  Get your sleep, whether it's 7 or 8 hours nightly. You know how much you need. And take a nap during the day. If your body is tired, take a 20-minute nap. Many studies have shown that taking a 20-minute nap increases productivity.

- **Allow for mistakes.** Reject the perfectionism claim that you must be perfect in everything and that everything must go according to plan. Life happens. So what?

- **Help someone.** Helping someone is a selfless act, and most often you actually get more than you give. Find someone or something and get involved, whether it's a local charity, such as the Girl Scouts or Boy Scouts, Big Brothers or Big Sisters, or a food pantry or a soup kitchen, or helping kids with special needs. Being involved in giving is a great stress reducer.

- **Make a decision to enjoy life.** Make this decision today, right now. Many people say, "Oh, I'll enjoy life during the weekends," or ". . . after this test is done," ". . . when the kids are out of the house," ". . . when I get this raise," or ". . . when I buy this house." Don't postpone making the decision to enjoy your life. Start today developing a mind-set that ultimately reduces stress. The payoff far outweighs the inaction.

Detachment and Fulfillment

We are a materials-based society that likes material things. Material possessions are nice, but they are not everything. You don't gain fulfillment by what you have, but rather by who you become. "If I buy this bigger house, I'll feel fulfilled. If I buy this luxury vehicle, it will really make me happy."

Stop searching for fulfillment through material possessions, because happiness is found in self-fulfillment. Find joy and beauty in simple things, like viewing a sunset, watching your child's baseball game, or developing relationships with loved ones. Self-fulfillment brings calmness and inner peace.

A life based on fulfillment through material possessions often leads to living in a higher degree of poverty. Although possessions may sustain you for a little while, you're left with only the possessions and an empty feeling. Attachments are never a replacement for the nurturing security that personal interactions can bring.

The more we are willing to let go of our attachments, the more powerful we become.

—Eva Gregory

Positive Ways to Start Your Day

There are many good ways to start your day and put yourself in charge, as well as protect you from the noise, chaos, and overstimulation going on around you. You can begin in silence by saying a prayer or reading a passage. Don't start your day by reading the newspaper or watching the news. Most of that information is depressing and only impedes your positive outlook.

Take an early morning walk or take time to write down your goals. Ask yourself some questions: "What did I do yesterday that brought me joy? What could I do today for someone else? What do I want to accomplish today? Where do I see myself one year from now?"

Starting your day in silence helps you develop strength to go forward and be productive in having a successful day.

We cannot place ourselves directly in God's presence without imposing upon ourselves interior and exterior silence. That is why we must accustom ourselves to stillness of the soul, of the eyes, of the tongue.

—Mother Teresa

12

Rewards of Self-Discipline

Leaders and the Military

Some of the best leaders come from our military institutions and schools across this country. One reason is because this environment teaches as well as cultivates self-discipline. They also have certain fitness requirements, which means people must keep themselves in good physical condition.

People at these institutions and schools must be up at a certain time and in class at a certain time. They must take tests, whether working on a degree or at their job. They must plan ahead, be diligent with their time, and know how to best use it, because many priorities are placed on them. They must be in control.

The military teaches and creates individuals with self-confidence, a key aspect in its ability to produce leaders. Sometimes when people enter the military, they are floundering between jobs or don't know exactly what they want to do with their life. But they leave with self-discipline and belief in themselves that they can do anything. Many military veterans go on to have success in other careers.

A friend named Derek, who was in his mid-20s, was hopping from job to job, not really sure of what he wanted to do with his life. He was sleeping on people's couches and didn't really have a plan or goal in mind. Then he decided to enlist in the Air Force and went to boot camp. At this writing, he has been there about two years, won some leadership awards, and is working to the rank of staff sergeant.

I have seen a miraculous turnaround in him, someone who is now a leader and whose confidence is through the roof. Derek can take a plan and execute it. His turnaround is totally 180 degrees in a positive direction.

It has been incredible to watch his transformation and see the type of person he has become. The military has helped instill that in him. I believe it was in him all along, but it took the right environment for him to become self-disciplined.

Seeking a Quick Fix

We live in a society where, when we want something—anything—we want it quickly, we want it now, and we don't want to wait for it. If you want something to eat at 2 AM, no problem, because McDonald's, Taco Bell, and Burger King are open 24 hours a day.

If you forget something, Walmart is open 24 hours a day in some locations. If your printer fails the day your paper is due, FedEx Office is open 24 hours daily.

Some people always seem to be looking for a quick fix and the latest, greatest new item. For example, losing weight is a billion-dollar industry, and almost every month a new diet pill comes out that everybody wants to take. And don't forget the latest book on how to lose weight. "My friend tried this and it worked for her."

I saw this firsthand when people came to me wanting to get in better shape. I told them: "It's going to come down to self-discipline. You must watch what you eat and make exercise a habit and a consistent part of your life. If you do those two things, then we'll look closer at making sure you get proper rest and chart your progress. If you combine all four of those aspects, then we'll be on our way."

Making real progress comes down to having self-discipline, but we see the opposite in our society. We see something and want the quick fix. We want to make $1 million, and we want to go from $0 to $1 million in one year.

Realize that if you build something fast, it's probably going to dissipate fast. But if you take time and build it slowly, there's a better chance that it will last longer.

If you lose 60 pounds in three months by trying some crazy workout or just drinking shakes or taking a pill, there's a strong chance you will gain back all the weight you lost. But if you lose a few pounds a month, chances are greater that you will keep that weight off for a long period of time.

Self-Discipline and Delayed Gratification

Colleague Joachim de Posada wrote *Don't Eat the Marshmallow,* and in it he tells a story of an experiment with young kids. Kids in a room were given two options. Either they could have one marshmallow right now, or they could have one marshmallow and wait a couple of minutes and then be given a second marshmallow.

It was often humorous to watch as kids agonized over this marshmallow. Some kids waited patiently and got a second marshmallow. Other kids quickly gobbled down one marshmallow and expected another one, but obviously didn't get it.

Follow-up with the kids showed that those who practiced delayed gratification and actually waited for the second marshmallow did much better in school and were more successful. Their test scores, their SATs, and their grades were a lot higher in middle school and high school.

This group also didn't have as many disciplinary problems as the other group. They somehow understood that if they waited and held off eating the first marshmallow, they would benefit.

That's what self-discipline teaches. It allows you to develop the discipline to hold off acting on impulse for immediate gratification and to be patient for something in the future. Self-discipline is about practicing self-control in order to reap a reward later.

It's Called Work

A fellow speaker and friend, Larry Winget, often says, "If your life sucks, it's because you suck." It's a pretty dramatic quote, but it refers to taking responsibility for your life and for your actions. In his book, *It's Called Work for a Reason!* Larry talks about work, and his message is so true.

Sometimes we think that just because someone is a success or makes a lot of money, maybe that person just got lucky or fell into his or her good fortune. That's rarely the case. Making money is the result of being a success.

At a speaking engagement in Marlborough, Massachusetts, I had some free time and drove over to Foxborough, home of the New England Patriots. At the time, the Patriots had won three Super Bowls under the direction of head coach Bill Belichick.

I walked around the Patriots complex and was amazed at how nice it was. Then I walked in the parking lot where the players' and coaches' cars were parked. It was autumn around 8:30 PM, and I saw "Head Coach, B. Belichick." And sure enough, his car was there. As I walked away, I was impressed by his dedication.

Here is a guy who has won three Super Bowls, and he was working late that night. One of the reasons they are so successful is because the coach puts in the work and the time. Be focused on the result and to get to your desired result you can't be afraid to work.

I'm sure that most people in the National Football League, coaches and players, would say that preparation is key and that you must put in the time if you want to be successful in any endeavor.

It's called "work" for a reason, and having self-discipline reinforces the ability to work hard and dedicate ourselves to achieving our ultimate goals.

Self-Discipline versus Regret

Most of us experience regret when we fail to exercise self-discipline over our actions, habits, and emotions. For example, taxes are due on April 15. Say you start in January, working 20 minutes one Saturday and an hour another Saturday. This habit continues until your taxes are done in March, and you avert any regret over not completing them.

If you said, "I'll do it this weekend," but kept putting it off because something kept coming up every weekend, when April 1 arrives and you've done nothing, you now feel deep regret. "Man, I wish I would have done this!"

As mentioned earlier, your high school reunion is approaching and you say to yourself, "I'd really like to lose 20 pounds." Disciplined behaviors would include going to the gym consistently, eating healthy foods, watching your calorie intake, and getting the proper amount of rest. But if you fail to perform those habits and it's the night before the reunion, you have regrets because you didn't exercise the self-discipline needed to reach your goal.

When you apply self-discipline, you avoid having regrets. You're not saying to yourself, "I wish I could have done this" or "I should have done this." Often, the regret you feel is more painful than the actual discipline.

Self-Discipline and Self-Image

A positive aspect of self-discipline is that, with practice, you start to develop a more positive self-image, seeing yourself in a different light as a person of action, as someone who follows through, or as a person of his or her word. Without self-discipline and self-control, you risk other people's negative opinions about you becoming reality and accepting it as the status quo.

For example, if someone says any of the following, sometimes we take such comments as truth due to low self-esteem: "You can't do this. You can go only so far. You can't live in that neighborhood. You will never be able to afford those houses. You're not that smart."

In recent years, Butler College in Indianapolis, Indiana, made it to the basketball championship games two years despite some expert opinions that, "They're just lucky to be in the tournament."

Nobody predicted they would go to the championship two years in a row. But they had such great self-discipline, in terms of practice, focus, and preparation, that they saw themselves in the championship game.

They knew their strengths, and what the so-called experts said or other coaches or players thought of them didn't matter. The only opinions that mattered were those of the coaches and players themselves. They developed a strong self-image through discipline in their practice sessions, in their collective focus, and in their overall preparations.

Self-image actually increases and becomes stronger when positive disciplinary practices are followed, overshadowing outside influences and opinions.

Self-Discipline and Sports Activities

Activities such as martial arts, basketball, football, soccer, karate, and gymnastics teach young people about self-discipline, which translates into work ethic. For example, playing a sport requires self-discipline; you have to go to practices and the games and must put in the time to become better.

"Life isn't fair" is a concept we sometimes try to shelter our young people from, but they discover it once they start competing in something like a sports activity.

Many students who participate in sports and other activities have higher grades than those who don't engage in sports or activities. As a high school athlete, my grades were often higher when I played a sport, because I had a limited amount of study time and had to be disciplined with my time; when I had all the time in the world, my grades suffered because I had too much time. In a sense, I was undisciplined with my time.

Start Somewhere

If you feel a bit overwhelmed at this point, start small and find a reasonable goal. For example, to improve your physical health, begin walking one day a week and gradually increase to two days a week. To improve your academics by reading more, read one chapter a week until you're ready for more.

Just do something small. Wherever you are currently in your goals, begin small and start to develop a higher level of motivation. Surrounding yourself with self-motivated people provides a great incentive to building your own motivation.

Andy Andrews, a speaking colleague, talks about a time in his life when he lived beneath a bridge and had a lot of time on his hands. He got a library card and read many biographies of people who had accomplished a great deal. He was inspired to do more and is now a top speaker. Be with self-motivated people and read books that inspire you.

The only difference between where you are now and where you'll be five years from now are the people you meet and the books you read.
—Charles "Tremendous" Jones

Just start somewhere. Start small and begin to develop a habit of self-discipline. Attend speaker events in your area and be around influential people who are driven, ambitious, and self-motivated. Surround yourself with people who have reached their destination, as well as those who continue to work on being self-motivated.

Consider what you watch on TV or see at the movies. As a kid in the fifth grade, I watched *Rudy* and said to myself: "If this guy can go to the premiere Catholic institution in the world and play football, I think I could go there. And even if I couldn't play football, maybe I could at least graduate from there." That inspired me to look further into attending. I also graduated from there.

Another movie that inspired me was *Walk the Line,* the story of country singer Johnny Cash. As a young man trying to find his way, he picked up a guitar and just went with it. His parents weren't musicians or wealthy, but he and his music influenced millions.

Self-Discipline in Business

Self-discipline teaches individuals to make sound business decisions through self-control and patience. Some of the tough times organizations go through can be attributed to people making hasty decisions, hoping to reap rewards in the short term rather than exercise the patience and self-discipline required for long-term success. Harris Rosen addressed this theme in a business article. He is the owner of seven hotels near Orlando, Florida, and he owns them free and clear. That means no debt, and this includes a $300 million hotel he opened in 2006.

Self-Discipline and Failure

Congratulations if you have decided to work toward a goal, but if you fail . . . so what? Nobody, and I mean nobody, has achieved anything great without failure. Failure holds a valuable lesson. It's a teaching tool that motivates you to get back up when you fall and to try again.

Suppose you decide to lose weight and work out once or twice a week. Then, maybe you skip a week and lose some of your desire because you get sidetracked with friends. Rather than think you have failed and stop completely, "Oh man, I failed, so now I can't do that," either pick up where you left off or restart your routine.

Realize that everyone fails at certain points of becoming successful. Just because you mapped out a course and decided to act on a decision, sometimes it just doesn't work out. Challenges come and go and occasional stumbling is inevitable.

Life happens, but self-discipline makes it possible to continue, and as you continue toward your goal, your sense of self-discipline also continues to grow. So don't be discouraged by failure. Most failures are temporary and hold only as much value as you permit them to hold.

Paying the Price for Success

It seems that some people don't want to pay the price for anything, much like the Entitlement Generation. When people in this generation enter the workforce, they want your job and they want it right now. They don't want to work 10 to 15 years to achieve their goals. But everything comes at a price, whether it's earning a six-figure salary or moving into that coveted corner office.

What price are you willing to pay for what you want? Are you willing to work the extra hours? Are you willing to spend the time it takes to become great? What are you willing to do?

In his book *Outliers,* Malcolm Gladwell talks about people with great success. Although some people seem to become an overnight success, in reality, they put in about 10,000 hours—or about eight years—to get there. Success rarely happens overnight, and it does come with a price.

At age 20, I gave my first paid speech, about 45 minutes long, in front of 950 high school students. Years later, I decided I wanted to be a top speaker in a seminar company, but I didn't assume I could just start out at the top. It took about three years before I made it to the top 1 percent, and I paid the price. You can reach the top in your organization a lot sooner. After I graduated I had to find my way to the seminar company but I was still going around speaking in some cases speaking for free.

Whatever price you pay for success, you must ask yourself, "Am I willing to pay that price?" And answer honestly. Self-discipline is the fuel and the engine to help you accomplish your goal.

When you develop self-discipline in one area of your life, the benefits spread to other areas and your confidence continually increases. You become a person who is consistent in actions, goals, and outcomes. You actually envision success and see yourself as being able to do anything.

Got PAPP?

When I give keynote speeches in front of large audiences, I sometimes bring T-shirts that say "Got Papp?" on the front and "**P**ersistence **A**lways **P**roduces **P**rosperity" on the back. The message is that when a wall goes up, you say: "I'm either going to go through that wall, I'm going to go over it, I'm going to go under it, or I'm going to go around it, but *I'm going to find a way to make it happen*."

What is your prosperity? Maybe it's in philanthropic endeavors and devoting your life to helping others through some type of service. Having a persistent mind-set produces the prosperity of living the good life—a fulfilled life and a successful life you know you are capable of living.

Nothing in the world can take the place of Persistence. Talent will not; nothing is more common than unsuccessful men with talent. Genius will not; unrewarded genius is almost a proverb. Education will not; the world is full of educated derelicts. Persistence and determination alone are omnipotent. The slogan "press on" has solved and always will solve the problems of the human race.

—Calvin Coolidge

Self-Discipline, Consistency, and Trust

A by-product of developing self-discipline is that you become consistent, and with consistency comes trust. When your organization displays self-discipline and is consistent in dealing with clients, it also becomes an organization that people trust.

Why do you go to your favorite restaurant? You go because it's good every night of the week, not just on Tuesday, Thursday, or Sunday. Why do I like Domino's pizza? Because it is consistently good, and I know what I'm getting, whether I'm in Pennsylvania, Georgia, Florida, or Michigan.

Self-discipline combined with consistency and trust is always a winning formula for success.

About the Author

E ric Papp has delivered professional training programs to corporate and private clients. He has been featured in the *New York Times, USA Today, Dallas Morning News,* and many other publications.

Eric received his BA at the University of Notre Dame. He was voted in the top 1 percent of management trainers in 2010. In addition to training and consulting, More than 80 percent of Eric's business comes from repeat customers. His partial client list:

- Utility Supply Management Alliance
- Million Dollar Round Table Florida Realtors
- Huntsman
- FEMA
- Nationwide

Leadership by Choice is a system designed for individuals and organizations to achieve personal greatness through four areas: leadership, communication, productivity, and personal development. He has taught thousands of people these practical applications. What are you waiting for?

www.ericpapp.com